# AN ATLAS OF
# TEXTUAL CRITICISM

T0382262

# CAMBRIDGE
## UNIVERSITY PRESS

University Printing House, Cambridge CB2 8BS, United Kingdom

Published in the United States of America by Cambridge University Press, New York

Cambridge University Press is part of the University of Cambridge.

It furthers the University's mission by disseminating knowledge in the pursuit of education, learning and research at the highest international levels of excellence.

www.cambridge.org
Information on this title: www.cambridge.org/9781107426931

© Cambridge University Press 1911

First published 1911
First paperback edition 2014

*A catalogue record for this publication is available from the British Library*

ISBN 978-1-107-42693-1 Paperback

# AN ATLAS OF
# TEXTUAL CRITICISM

BEING AN ATTEMPT TO SHOW THE
MUTUAL RELATIONSHIP OF THE
AUTHORITIES FOR THE TEXT
OF THE NEW TESTAMENT
UP TO ABOUT 1000 A.D.

BY

EDWARD ARDRON HUTTON, M.A.
VICAR OF ST MICHAEL'S, HARGRAVE

Cambridge:
at the University Press
1911

כִּי־עִמְּךָ מְקוֹר חַיִּים
בְּאוֹרְךָ נִרְאֶה־אוֹר

Toil at the sacred text ;
More fruitful grows the field ;
Each generation for the next
Prepares a richer yield.

TO THE MEMORY OF

# SIR THOMAS MOULSON

A NATIVE OF HARGRAVE, WHO BECAME ALDERMAN,
SHERIFF AND LORD MAYOR OF LONDON. HE BUILT
AND ENDOWED ST MICHAEL'S CHURCH, HARGRAVE,
AND TO HIS BOUNTY AND MUNIFICENCE THE AUTHOR
OF THIS WORK HAS BEEN FOR MANY YEARS INDEBTED.


"The Lord grant unto him that he may find mercy of the
Lord in that day." Amen.

" *I would have everyone write what he knows, and as much as he knows, but no more; and that not in this only, but in all other subjects. For such a person may have some particular knowledge and experience of the nature of such a person or such a fountain, that as to other things, knows no more than what everybody does, and yet, to keep a clutter with this little pittance of his, will undertake to write the whole body of physicks; a vice from whence great inconveniences derive their original.*"

MONTAIGNE.

# PREFACE

THE object of this book is threefold. First it is intended to be a kind of Atlas to any modern critical text of the New Testament, such as *Tregelles*, *Alford*, and above all, *Tischendorf*. Hence their nomenclature has been retained, and the reader will find "Coptic" where he might expect Bohairic, "Philoxenian" for Harklean, and a few other terms such as "Ambrosiaster" etc. To ask a student to read critical notes and to form his own conclusions, is to give a blind sailor a compass and expect him to find port. This book, therefore, is intended to be a kind of chart to show the student his way in what at first seems a veritable maze, for "Knowledge of Documents must precede judgement of readings."

Secondly, it is intended to be an atlas to modern works on textual criticism. The tables form admirable tests whereby to prove the truth or otherwise of many of the statements made in such text books, and such statements may at once be brought to book and approved or rejected.

Let us take the following from Scrivener's Introduction (Vol. I. p. 162) where the author is speaking of Codex Ξ.

"In the 564 places wherein Tischendorf cites it in his eighth edition, it supports Cod. L in full three cases out of four, and those the most characteristic. It stands alone only 14 times, and with Cod. L or others against the five great uncials only 30 times. In regard to these latter, Cod. Ξ sides plainly with Cod. B in preference to Cod. A, following B alone 7 times, BL 24 times, but ℵ 13 times, A 15 times, C (which is often defective) 5 times, D 14 times, with none of these unsupported except with ℵ once. Their combinations in agreement with Ξ are curious and complicated, but lead to the same result. This copy is with ℵB 6 times, with ℵBL 55; with ℵBC 20, but with ℵBD as many as 54 times, with ℵBCD 38 times; with BCD thrice, with BC six times, with BD 13. It combines with ℵA 10 times, with AC 15, with AD 11, with ℵAC 16, with ACD 12, with ℵAD six, with ℵACD twelve. Thus Cod. Ξ favours B against A 226 times, A against B 97. Combinations of its readings opposed to both A and B are ℵC six, ℵD eight, CD two, ℵCD three. In the other passages it favours ABC against ℵD eleven times, ABCD against ℵ eight times, ℵABC against D eighteen times, ℵABD against C, or where C is defective, 39 times, and is expressly cited 27 times as standing with ℵABCD against later copies. The character of the variations of Cod. Ξ from the Received text may be judged of by the estimate made by some scholar, that 47 of them are transpositions in the order of the words, 201 are substitutions of one word for another, 118 are omissions, while the additions do not exceed 24 (Christian Remembrancer, Jan. 1862)."

This extract must have cost many hours of labour and is an apt illustration of that "multiplying words without knowledge" that has been the curse of textual criticism ever since Mill set the example in his verbose prolegomena. Who for instance can determine the exact relationship of Ξ from the above? Compare the whole with my tables and the superiority of the latter will be at once seen.

Here is another taken from the same source (Vol. I. p. 144). He is speaking of P and Q.

" As regards their text we observe that in the first hundred verses of St Luke which are contained in both copies, wherein P is cited for various readings 216 times, and Q 182 times, P stands alone 14 times, Q not once. P agrees with other manuscripts against AB 21 times, Q 19: P agrees with AB united 50 times, Q also 50: P sides with B against A 29 times, Q 38 : but P accords with A against B in 102 places, Q in 75."

Here the statement is more simply put and something may be gathered, but not until we know that B is an Alexandrine text and A one mainly Syrian. A glance at the chart of St Luke will tell all this and much more.

Of itself the extract is worthless till we know the mutual relationship of A and B.

But these are not the chief object of this work. Scattered throughout Europe and the East we have about 4000 Greek MSS. of the New Testament. We know the text of nearly all the uncials, but of the cursives we know thoroughly perhaps only a tenth or even less. The rest lie at our national or other libraries in glass cases or locked presses and are shown merely as specimens of caligraphy or illumination, and the cicerone directs our attention to them as "curiosities" like the lantern of Guy Fawkes or that wonderful threepenny bit that "Bodley" Coxe (may he rest in peace) once used as a touchstone to divide the sheep from the goats.

And amongst them lie one per cent., perhaps, of priceless texts like 61 (Acts) or 17 (Pauline Epistles) and our latest Greek Testament comes out with nearly 3000 passages marked as still uncertain.

What is really wanted is a thorough preliminary survey of every MS. and such a survey can only be made by collating them in a uniform series of specially selected passages which, if numerous enough, would give us a perfect idea of their mutual relationship. General ideas are of no value whatever. We must have exactness and this can only be secured by submitting all alike to the same process and such is the object of the present work. It merely goes down to about

1000 A.D., but material exists for much more in the exact collations of Scrivener, Matthaei, Alter, Reiche and others, and all these and others the author has in hand and hopes, if possible, to publish.

Nor is the task hopeless or a chimera. We know that Kennicott alone collated 581 MSS. of the Old Testament (of which 102 contained the whole) and that he and De Rossi together collated:

490 MSS. of Genesis
549    „    the Megilloth
495    „    the Psalms
172    „    Ezra and Nehemiah
211    „    the Chronicles.

It is quite beyond one man's power to do the work, but a dozen or a score would soon finish it. I mean, of course, comparatively soon.

Let me give an instance of the usefulness of such a work as will appeal at least to some of my readers. Professor Von Soden has given us list after list of readings of MSS. and groups. These lists are not only a weariness to the flesh but are based often upon the mere peculiarities of each group. Suppose one uniform set of readings had been chosen whereby to test all alike I venture to think we should have obtained far more insight into the mutual relationship of the documents. At present they are each divided into their groups, but the relationship of each group to the other documents is often all but impossible to determine. I say this in no carping spirit. I cannot but attest my great respect to the enormous work enshrined in these lists. My sole contention is that a uniform standard is after all far better than mere idiosyncrasies, and I do not fear to assert my conviction that every reader of the Professor's work will agree with me.

To collate texts of the Syrian family is altogether unnecessary. We probably know it quite as well as the text of Shakespeare. But to find out the other texts is indispensable if textual criticism is not to stand still. It is to facilitate this work that the Appendix is so arranged as to be of practical use for this purpose. Space is left under each reading for insertion of reference number etc. of MSS. and, besides the usual chapter and verse, the κεφαλαῖα numbers are also given and the place in the section (where necessary) is inserted in the form of a decimal so that there can seldom be much difficulty in finding the place. The Appendix to Chapter III (Vol. I) of Scrivener will be found an essential guide in the case of *Evangelisteria* and Bruder's *Concordance* will be of much use in the Acts and Epistles where the divisions are longer. It will be found that the decimals are usually quite sufficient. Where no decimal occurs the passage is at the very beginning of the section, or the section is too short to need such aid.

The selection of readings are given in full in the

Appendix and suggestions as to alterations will be welcomed. I am quite convinced that no selection of passages will afford anything but confirmation of my tables and conclusions, and he who will carefully analyse a single chapter of any book of the New Testament will find there an answer to any criticisms that he may be inclined to make or may have read.

Many will think it strange that no mention is made of Professor Von Soden or of Professor Weiss. The author makes no excuse for this. This little work has not for its object the criticism of others and this has been avoided as much as possible. Moreover there is the further question of whether the author is competent to criticise the Professors. The author at any rate doubts it. Wearisome as many of Professor Von Soden's lists are to read there can be little doubt that some of them shed important light on the relationship between many of our authorities and will be found of much use to students.

Before concluding I must not forget to acknowledge my indebtedness to the advantages afforded to me by several visits to St Deiniol's Library, Hawarden, and especially to the courtesy and kindness of the Warden, Dr Joyce. I feel I owe much to the munificence of Mr Gladstone and his family and I here own my indebtedness.

To Dr Swete I owe thanks on account of one or two queries put to him as President of the Central Society for Sacred Study, which he answered both promptly and fully.

The revision of the Appendix I owe to the kindness of my nephew Robert Jermyn Hutton of St John's College, Cambridge. It would perhaps not become me to say more of a near relation than that I have every confidence in both his competence and his accuracy.

Above all I owe most to Professor F. C. Burkitt who although personally quite unknown to me kindly consented to read my MS. To him I am indebted for a number of suggestions and corrections all of which are incorporated in the text and tables as far as possible in Professor Burkitt's own words. It must be distinctly understood that in no way is Professor Burkitt responsible either for the accuracy of the tables or for any opinions expressed by me. His responsibility ends with his amendments and suggestions. Faults still remaining are the author's and his only. To Professor Burkitt I am also indebted for the loan of Père Batiffol's edition of Codex $\phi$ and for Belsheim's edition of 565 with the corrections made by the Rev. H. S. Cronin.

Friends tell me that some will think the notes too "scrappy." If this be the case let them reflect that my aim has been as far as possible not to trench on the usual manuals, nor repeat what has been better said elsewhere. The reader is expected to study the tables, and not the letter press, the latter being unavoidable but by all means to be kept down.

I do not ask any critic to spare me. I do ask the reader to believe that this work is not the outcome of a sudden resolution to rush into print, nor like the prophet's gourd, the growth of a single night. Twenty-four years ago I wrote a paper pointing out the peculiarities of L, of Δ and of 17 (Pauline Epp.) and sent it to the *Guardian* and *The Expositor* by both of whom it was returned, so that I have at any rate had time for reflection, and I may add for work, at the subject.

No one can learn textual criticism from reading alone, any more than chemical analysis can be learned from books only. The student must buy a drawing board and some sheets of squared paper and work out the problems for himself. I can assure him that the tables here given do not tell everything, and that much reward awaits him.

But do not let me again forget the real object of this work, namely to urge an immediate preliminary survey on the lines laid down, of every Greek MS. whose text is not known. A few years would here bring an immense harvest and put the Greek Testament on a level such as men have hitherto only imagined. The work is for a younger generation. It is sufficient to have been the preacher of a crusade though one can never hope perhaps to take an active part.

And here I leave it, not without hopes that my work may be of some use if only to beginners. If it serves others also I shall be more than satisfied. It has been in a true sense a labour of love, and has occupied many hours that might have been less profitably employed. My one hope is that it may serve the special object with which it has been written. In any case, Deo solum sit gloria, " quia exaltatum est nomen ejus solius, gloria ejus in caelo et in terrâ."

E. ARDRON HUTTON.

HARGRAVE,
   *The Feast of the Epiphany*, 1911.

# CONTENTS

available for download from www.cambridge.org/9781107426931

# ERRATA

p. 13, line 4, *for* eighteen *read* seventeen.
p. 26, line 27, for *g* read *h*.

# INTRODUCTION

IT is much to be regretted that the textual criticism
of the New Testament is not by any means a favourite study. Few people of themselves take it up, and
fewer still know its usefulness or its fascination. Most
people vote it dry and dreary, and far from numerous
are they who love textual criticism for its own sake.
Others there are whose chief interest is in the so-called
higher criticism, or more often in the simple exegesis
required for sermons and the like. These will often
take some modern critical text for standard, and care
nothing for its history or value. And yet one cannot
help thinking that such might well remember Dr Routh's
reply when asked for the name of the best commentary.
" The Vulgate, young man, the Vulgate." He who
studies the critical notes in Tischendorf will often find
them of immense value. In the Epistle to the Romans
for instance there is not a single chapter where light is
not shed both by the versions and by the pithy translations of some of the Fathers. And in all the Epistles
and elsewhere real gems will frequently be found where
we instinctively feel that the very word has been hit
upon by those unknown translators and by the Fathers.

Others look upon the subject as offering little scope
for new and original study. This, however, is by no
means the case. Take for instance the Greek MSS.,

and we find that the uncials only have been thoroughly collated, and that of the thousands of cursives a twentieth at the most are available to the critic, though many exist which are known to possess exceptional value.

The Versions have not only been attacked, but much and very valuable work has been accomplished, especially by our own countrymen. We have now editions of all the Four Gospels in the Old Syriac, the Peshitta, the Bohairic, and the Gothic, and of the Vulgate in both the Gospels and the Acts. We have besides these continuous texts of every one of the Old Latin MSS., together with the Philoxenian Apocalypse. Still, even here we have lacunae that obviously offer scope for much work.

As regards the Fathers, much too has been done of late years, and the Berlin Corpus for the Greek, and the Vienna Corpus for the Latin, fulfil all the requirements of the critic, and the number of passages where doubt exists as to the exact form of text quoted must now be very few.

There is, however, another field in which work must perforce be done by all who would become adepts in New Testament study. Most students find, after reading the usual manuals and introductions, that something more is required on entering upon the actual study of a critical edition of the Greek text. The knowledge so far acquired is not always helpful, and the so-called canons of criticism too often seem inapplicable or even mutually antagonistic.

This is seen more especially when such a text as Scrivener's Greek Testament is studied or referred to, since in numerous passages it will be found that whilst one critic supports a reading, another as decisively rejects it, while perhaps the remainder relegate it to the margin, or direct attention to its doubtfulness by a star or a dagger or by a variety of brackets and signs too numerous to mention.

The question at once arises as to the cause of the doubt, and what is its real or probable value. We may perhaps conclude that these differences arise from the idiosyncrasies of critics, or from mere bias or prejudice on their part for particular authorities, and we ask— when judges differ, who shall decide? This is, however, not the attitude of the thoughtful student, or even of common sense. Even when judges differ we may at least resift the evidence for ourselves and form an opinion as to the reasonableness of their doubts. And in textual criticism, where the evidence is not personal but documentary and so largely mechanical, we may surely do the same. This, however, throws us back on the evidence itself, and we are at once confronted with the question as to the individual and combined value of the authorities and their mutual independence and relationship.

Fortunately the latter problem is by no means insoluble, and since the former will be found to largely depend on the latter, we may leave out for awhile all questions as to value and excellence whilst we examine the other question as to the mutual relationship of the documents concerned.

More than a hundred years ago it was pointed out by Griesbach that most of our authorities fall into three chief groups or families, which he named the Alexandrine, the Western, and the Byzantine, and though later critics have made rearrangements or subdivided these groups into smaller, yet few critics now question the existence of these three great groups. No argument must be built on the names themselves, nor do we for the present maintain their appropriateness or the reverse. Our object is to divide the available mass of textual material into their different groups or recensions. The valuation of each of them can be obtained only by a subsequent and different process.

Fortunately for our purpose a large number of passages exist where the three families offer mutually conflicting evidence, and it is quite obvious to the reader that by a careful collation of such we can separate our authorities and find out how far mixture interferes with their evidence.

It is unfortunately impossible to include every triple reading in the tables, but as far as possible every reading has been included that was without doubt and ambiguity. In other words our aim has been to include rather than exclude, and every triple reading has been carefully examined previous to insertion or rejection. Rejected readings fall in the main into one of the following classes.

(*a*) Readings of extreme difficulty that must be reserved to the very last stage. These are comparatively few in number. In each case the evidence is so conflicting or scanty, and the various authorities in such confusion, that summary decision is impossible.

(*b*) Readings where a mere variation of tense or the addition of a pronoun is in question. In these cases the Versions often use the tense which makes the best translation, and both Versions and Fathers add and omit pronouns at their will. (Cf. the italics of the A.V.) The Latin Versions often translate a Greek imperfect by the perfect when the latter seems to better express the sense (as indeed might be expected), whilst some

Versions are unable to discriminate between the imperfect and the aorist.

(*c*) Readings where the order of the Greek words is in question and where, therefore, the evidence of the Versions cannot be adduced.

(*d*) There still remain a comparatively small number of cases that cannot be classified, but where, from one cause or another, the evidence of the Versions or Fathers cannot be adduced, and which, therefore, have been omitted. It is believed that a sifting of the evidence will justify to the reader the judgment of the writer. In any case the number of these is so small that they cannot make any appreciable difference in the final result. It seemed best to leave them out rather than to be too hasty.

Before examining the triple readings the student should go through a chapter or two of each great division of the Greek Testament in order to obtain a fair general knowledge of the groups into which the witnesses fall. A score or so of readings taken all but at random will show that one small group exists of which B and ℵ are the most constant members. Another small group contains (in the Gospels) D as its most frequent representative, whilst a very large group exists which is generally arrayed in direct opposition to both the former. Each of these groups includes lesser groups, but the differences between the members of each group are very small compared to the differences between the groups themselves. The groups are as distinct as the white from the negro, the lesser groups are perhaps as distinct as a Frenchman from ourselves.

Whilst we are thus dividing the witnesses into their several families we may at the same time try to discover

which of these families is the best. This is obviously
the next stage, and unfortunately cannot be ascertained
by a merely mechanical process, but each must use his
own personal judgment, and the process only can be
indicated.   Here, therefore, the honesty of the reader
will become an important factor.

Let us suppose that we have drawn a fairly distinct
line of division and separated our documents into three
great classes.   If we now ask which of these classes
is likely to be the best, we should probably answer that
the best would probably satisfy the following tests :

(*a*)   It would have the support of the oldest of the
witnesses.

(*b*)   It would have the support of the widest geographical area, i.e. it would have attestation from all parts
of the early Christian world, and not from one area only.

(*c*)   It would approve itself to us as the best.   These
tests, however, are not as easy to apply as might at first
sight appear.   It will be of considerable assistance to us
to compile a list of Fathers and Versions arranged in
geographical divisions and chronological order.   The
geographical divisions may be Africa, Alexandria,
Jerusalem, Antioch and Syria, Byzantium and Asia
Minor, Rome and the West.   Since the dates of the
Fathers and Versions are fairly well known there is
little difficulty in doing this.

The Syriac and Latin Versions may be left by themselves in order that the student may investigate for
himself their place of origin.

The first test, that of antiquity, is not so decisive as
we might wish.   Passing over the Apostolic Fathers
and a few early remains (like the Didache) where the
quotations are too few for judgment, we find as soon as

we come to Justin Martyr and Marcion, that Western readings are frequent, and about the same time we have continuous Western texts in the Old Syriac, the Old Latin, and Tatian. From thence onwards to about A.D. 250 we have a number of Fathers, all of whom, except Origen, are mainly Western. The great gap in the Fathers during the whole of the latter half of the third century makes it impossible to follow continuously the lines of descent, but by the Nicene period we find confusion worse confounded, and readings have sprung up of which the earlier texts give not a trace, till in St Chrysostom we find the late Syrian text appearing. Thus the test of antiquity is decidedly against the Syrian, and as decidedly in favour of the Western and Alexandrine. In spite of the large number of Fathers with Western texts we find that when express citations are made "from old copies" and the like, such quotations are in a large majority of cases Alexandrine. The Western text was thus in use, both in the Church and privately, and yet it was known to be corrupt, hence the citation of the older and different text. It is a contemporary testimony to the excellence of the Alexandrine text that cannot be overlooked, and must not be forgotten.

It will probably have been gathered from the last paragraph that the second test is of little practical use since before the end of the second century all Christendom was flooded with Western MSS., and only here and there do we find any other. Width of attestation is therefore no proof of excellence. All that can be said is that where wide attestation to a Western reading prevails it is what we might expect, whilst in other cases the contrary is the case. In the latter case only could it have any value.

The third test does not mean that we are simply to compare the three readings and pick out the best according to our individual unaided judgment. On the contrary, we must bring each to the test offered by those rules of internal evidence that apply equally to sacred and to secular texts. Perhaps the best *résumé* of these will be found in Alford's Greek Testament (Vol. I. Ch. VI. Sec. I, par. 19), and this at least ought to be thoroughly mastered. The result of such comparisons is all but universally in favour of the Alexandrine text. We may sometimes be obliged to suspend judgment, but seldom indeed will the student give a decided verdict for either the Western or the Syrian reading.

Thus we find the first test on the whole favourable to the Western and Alexandrine text, but seldom or never to the Syrian. The second test most often favours the Western, and again never the Syrian, whilst the third is all but universally favourable to the Alexandrine.

The bearing of all this is obvious, for whilst it cannot be denied that the Syrian text often adopts an ancient reading, and very often a Western one, yet scarcely a single Ante-Nicene Father or Version has any knowledge of such a text. It must be therefore discarded altogether as too late for all purposes of practical criticism. Dr Kenyon has given a good example of a similar rejection of all but two or three MSS. in the case of Sophocles where the total number of authorities is over a hundred, and in the classics this is by no means an isolated case. It is true that rejection of the Syrian text reduces us at most to but a score of authorities, and that of these the Western, who number more than three-fourths, must often be rejected too, but this cannot be helped.

The question is not one of numbers but of value, and here criticism is decisive.

Our final text must therefore often be difficult of determination, and here Drs Westcott and Hort have shown their wisdom in giving a much larger number of alternative readings than any other critic, and thus better representing the present state of New Testament criticism. In other words, while the principles of criticism are satisfactory enough, the paucity of authorities makes it unsafe to be too confident in all cases. Hesitation is the truest wisdom, and in the New Testament best represents the present state of the case. Infallibility is the mark of the ignoramus, or of the charlatan.

A few words seem to be required on the question as to whether bias or prejudice has in any way vitiated the tables or the opinions formed as to the results thus obtained. It is obvious that the author is the worst person possible to discuss these points, but still something must be attempted and the rest left to the reader's judgment.

Prejudices may be of two kinds, viz. a predilection for one of the families or predilection for one or more authorities.

Now as regards families the author has made it quite plain that he believes the Alexandrine family to best represent the original text. This opinion is shared by most critics. But this is only a general opinion, and since the Alexandrine witnesses are few and not always unanimous it is impossible at the present day to accept every such reading. Principles of criticism may be right, but material may be wanting and evidence insufficient. A frank suspension of judgment will in such cases be wisest.

In the case of the tables in this book it is difficult to see how such predilection can vitiate results as no decision as to the final merit of any reading has anything to do with their place in the tables. A reading is Alexandrine by attestation of certain witnesses, and whether in itself good, bad or indifferent is entered as such in the tables, which thus contain readings that may nevertheless be far from being *ipso facto* genuine and certainly very far from being always acceptable when judged by internal evidence, i.e. subjective criticism, with which for the present we have nothing to do.

It is hoped that this point will be seen, and that by adopting documentary evidence only the effect of any prejudice or preference may have been fully discounted.

The other point is however of very much more importance and must be fully discussed.

Nearly thirty years ago the author began his studies with full belief in the comparative excellence of ℵ, which, however, soon changed, and from that time onwards he has had no reason to doubt that B is the better and far more reliable as a representative of the Alexandrine text. And yet B is human and far from perfect, and its singular and even subsingular are often open to grave question.

No doubt B now and then stands out as having obviously the right reading unsupported though it may be by other members of its own class, but in no case has a reading been inserted in the tables as Alexandrine when supported by it alone, and in nearly every case the Alexandrine readings in all the tables have the support of Tischendorf, Westcott and Hort, Tregelles, the Revisers, and usually of that excellent, and cautious critic Dean Alford.

It is hoped that such a course may have eliminated the effect of this second kind of prejudice. It is difficult to see what further precautions could have been taken in view of the fact that the comparatively pure Alexandrine authorities are never more than half a dozen and sometimes only half that number. The point to be noticed is that the secondary attestation is sensibly the same however many or few the primary may be, and that moreover the other families are still supported by the same members as before in either case. This shows that the principles of selection have been fairly consistently carried out in all cases. If the value of B as an Alexandrine authority be rated as 100 the corresponding value of א is probably about 90 and of L about 85. Z and one or two others are quite equal to א if not superior, but such figures are only rough estimates and must be taken as such.

# THE HOLY GOSPELS

IT is hoped that the tables appended will be more or less self-explanatory. The notes therefore which we here add will be confined to the more important or to the less obvious points. Reference will be made twice to a similar analysis of pure Syrian readings in which above 500 readings are tabulated in the Gospels alone and which, if a favourable reception be accorded to the present work, will in due course be published. The allusions here made do not require actual knowledge of them.

The tables, it will be seen, show at once the relationships of the different witnesses. A cross (×) signifies an Alexandrine reading, a dash (/) a Western, whilst a dot denotes a Syrian.

Where P is found some peculiar reading is denoted, whilst a blank signifies either non-existence or now and then differences between the different editors. Here and there a few changes to a more correct reading have been made on the authority of modern editions of the Versions and from *Texts and Studies* and the like publications. Such alterations are few, and for all practical purposes the quotations may be taken as those of Tischendorf, Tregelles and Alford.

It will be seen that the Alexandrine division is peculiarly weak, the only pure members being ℵ and B. The most striking result is that shown by L, which is seen to be nearly pure Syrian for the first eighteen chapters of St Matthew. The following table gives an analysis of its text in the case of pure Syrian readings:

|  | Times quoted | Syrian | Non-Syrian |
|---|---|---|---|
| St Matt. to end of Chap. xvii. | 68 | 55 | 13 |
| „ xviii. to end . . | 49 | 7 | 42 |
| St Mark . . . . | 117 | 4 | 113 |
| St Luke . . . . | 160 | 1 | 159 |
| St John . . . . | 129 | 14 | 115 |

In St Mark the Syrian readings are all at the beginning, the last tabulated being at iii. 8. In St John the Syrian readings seem to be evenly divided. We must therefore claim for L a primary position amongst the Alexandrine group. Even its Syrian readings (omitting the pure Syrian portion) may be ancient readings afterwards adopted by the Syrian text.

The case of Δ is somewhat similar to L. It has usually been thought to have an Alexandrine text throughout the whole of St Mark. This however is not so. The first two chapters of St Mark are Syrian, and the Syrian recommences at the beginning of Chapter xii. The intervening Chapters iii. to xii. (both inclusive) alone contain the Alexandrine text. The following is the analysis of Syrian readings in St Mark:

|  | Quoted | Syrian | Non-Syrian |
|---|---|---|---|
| St Mark i.—ii. . . . . | 11 | 7 | 4 |
| „ iii.—xii. (incl.) . . | 92 | 3 | 89 |
| „ xiii.—end . . . | 17 | 12 | 5 |

It will be noticed that the text of C is best in

St Mark and St John. In this it is followed by 565 and one or two more of the cursives. As regards those authorities quoted but a few times all that can be now said is as follows:

Ξ, Z (T is nearly pure) are pure Alexandrine.

P, Y are pure Syrian.

Q, R are mixed texts.

The comparatively small but important group of mixed MSS. of the Gospels has never yet been satisfactorily accounted for and it is to be feared that they are all summarily dismissed as of little value or interest. Thus they are left out of account or, as Dr Scrivener complained, and as was partially true in his days, they are quoted when they agree with ℵ or B or D, etc., but ignored when they differ from these and support the later uncials. This is obviously unfair and infringes the first and greatest of all canons of criticism, which is that all evidence must be taken into account. We propose therefore to consider the two points of primary importance, namely the origin and the value of mixed texts. We shall confine our remarks to the Gospels as the most important and also as containing better material for our investigation than the remainder of the New Testament.

Here we have codex 1 and its allies, 13 and its companions, besides 22, 28, 157, 565, 700 and others of lesser note.

The first point of importance that we must make is to point out that in nearly all cases MSS. are not mere mechanical transcripts of previous copies but the work of men with an intimate knowledge of their New Testament. Even when we come to obvious copies the same thing applies and alterations are made that show intelligence at work. The best examples are F and G in the Pauline Epistles where, neglecting itacisms, etc., we have about 200 real various readings or two per chapter, a marked example of how unmechanical transcription may be and probably often was.

In order to make the matter plain we will take an instance where the facts are absolutely undisputed. The Old Latin Gospels were revised by Jerome in A.D. 384. One result was that the experiment was tried of putting new wine into old bottles, and we get a number of Old Latin MSS. revised by comparison with the Vulgate, and thus neither the one nor the other, moreover not one of even the best Vulgate MSS., has escaped contamination from the more ancient version. This is exactly what we might expect and what we invariably find in all such cases. The one before us is however complicated by the fact that all the non-African MSS. of the Old Latin (i.e. all except *k, e,* and *m*), have also been affected by revision into conformity with either the Alexandrine or the Syrian text, and that previous to the Vulgate mixture being introduced.

Now we turn to Greek MSS. for instances of similar processes in actual progress, and have not far to seek.

Two groups of MSS. have been well known for some time—(one the Ferrar group, the other Codex 1 and its allies). The members of the Ferrar group are so closely related that we cannot but conclude that their common ancestor is not many generations from any of them. The other group is less closely related and the interest in tracing out its genealogy is therefore the greater. As 131 is not a member of the group save in St Mark up to v. 26 and in St Luke (except the last chapter) we must take our examples from these portions. Like Δ

the MS. 131 seems to have been copied from a muti-
lated archetype and the lacunae filled up from a Syrian
text.

We will first take St Mark up to v. 26. We notice
that most variations are taken from a Syrian text. The
non-Syrian peculiarities of 118 and 131 are few and
unimportant. 209 has no peculiarities worth notice.

We analyse their common readings and find that
118, 131 and 209 are in agreement with the Syrian text
six times only in 78 citations. This is a very small
proportion indeed, being only one in 13. There was
therefore but little Syrian corruption in their common
ancestor who was probably removed from 1 by but a
single generation, its total corruption being less than
8 per cent.

We now turn to the pairs and find

   118 and 131 together 15 times
   118 and 209  „  16 „
   131 and 209  „  0 „

This too is very significant and tells its own tale.
The ancestors of 131 and 209 diverge altogether in this
generation whilst the ancestor of 118 is equally related
to both. I say ancestors because we are not yet arrived
at any of the MSS. themselves.

The next step is a study of the singular readings
where we find

   118 alone 20 times
   131 „  20 „
   209 „  1 „

Thus 209 has come down unaltered from the second
generation whilst 118 and 131 have both received new
and independent accretions of Syrian readings.

With these analyses we may proceed to construct a

genealogical tree which would be perfect except for the fact that in the course of the different Syrian additions many of the Syrian readings must have been the same in all the cases except in the peculiar readings.

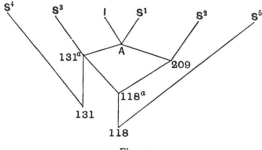

Fig. 1.

The original of the whole series (as far as our knowledge goes) is 1. This plus S¹ (the first borrowing from a Syrian source) gives us A the ancestor of all our present representatives of the family. A plus another Syrian accretion (S³) gives us the ancestor of 131 (here called 131ᵃ) whilst A + S² gives us 209 itself. And so we go on. It is nothing to the point to say that the relative ages of the MSS. do not agree with the tables. By 118, 131 and 209 we mean not our present actual MSS. but their prototypes which may be any century as far as our present knowledge goes.

Such a genealogy gives us no information about 1 itself because no genealogies can go further than historical records justify. In the case before us the number of waves of corruption is rather smaller than we might expect and each of them is comparatively small also. This may be accounted for by our having only four MSS. in all and our having exhausted all the combinations of those four. The genealogical table shows that all the MSS. are corruptions of 1 and thus can all be wiped out as far as witness to a pre-Syrian text is concerned.

This last conclusion is so important that it seemed worth testing. We therefore took another passage from the middle of St Luke's Gospel—chapters viii. ix. and x. —where all four MSS. are available and which is exactly the same length (10 pages) as the other in Professor Lake's book.

The Syrian readings common to all these three are 21 out of a total of 69—a far closer relationship than before. The common archetype of all three was therefore itself greatly corrupted.

The readings common to two are:

118 and 131   2 readings

118 and 209  20   „

131 and 209   0   „

Thus 118 and 209 are quite independent of 131, whilst 118 is again closely related to 209.

The peculiarities are as follows:

Peculiar to 118  10

„    „  131  16

„    „  209   0

The genealogy is thus rather simpler than before

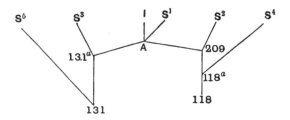

Fig. 2.

118[a] was a copy of 209 which was afterwards corrupted by S[4] and produced 118. The two readings
common to 118 and 131 have been neglected as mere
coincidences.

It is not possible to make much more of these figures.
In what has been said it will be recognised by some that
my conclusions are exactly the same as Professor Lake's
in St Luke and not quite the same in St Mark. It is
probable that this latter is owing either to the shortness
of the passage or to that anomalous position that St Mark's
text shows in many MSS. and amongst them in 1. 118 is
all but a copy of 209 in St Luke and very closely related
to it in St Mark.

The real point to be noticed is that successive waves
of Syrian corruption have taken place, and no one would
for a moment try to restore the text of 1 by means of
agreement between the other three.

And doubtless what here took place happened in
most cases. When the Syrian text began to be taken
as authoritative other texts would be brought more or
less into conformity with it—some less, like 33, 565
(St Mark), 700, 61 (Acts), and others more, like 13 and
its fellows, or still more 28, 22, 157 and a few others,
until finally we get MSS. like KΠ with but a small
pre-Syrian element. The chief importance of all these
is that they are proofs that many of the readings of א,
B and D are not peculiarities of those MSS. but real
readings which were once current just as in fact non-
Vulgate readings in mixed Latin texts are of value as
corroboration of the purer Western texts.

We can easily imagine that this is exactly what
would happen as soon as an authorized text once gained
respect. The old MSS. would be corrected by the neces-

sary additions or omissions, but many things, such as differences of order, would be left unaltered as of little importance and thus a mixed text with a good basis would go forth to be again altered into greater conformity by subsequent generations until the trace of the original exemplar was all but lost. Besides these we should have of course perfect copies of the new authorized text and these would gradually overwhelm the others just as MSS. of the Vulgate slowly got the upper hand of the mixed texts. The processes were exactly the same and the result was similar in both cases.

But this is not all. What critics hope to find in mixed MSS. is a clue or clues to much of the past history of the text, and this search is not so hopeless as it seems. For instance we have a small but exceedingly important little group of authorities that at present are grouped with greatly differing MSS. under the general head of Western. This group consists of the Old Syriac (both MSS.), *e, k, m* of the Old Latin and probably the Sahidic. To this group we cannot at present add a single Greek MS. though it has the support of D on the whole. But it is not at all impossible that some day a MS. hitherto overlooked may turn out to be at least the connecting link between this grouplet and the Western family, and even if it were not pure its value would be considerable. "Missing links" are always useful whether in geology or here.

Nor is this at all an imaginary case. In the Acts for instance we have this very thing, and its value no one can overestimate. There we have a small group of mixed MSS. composed of 137, 214 (a^scr) and 216 (c^scr). We had before their discovery merely the Harklean and D witnessing, in the main, to a large number of peculiar readings with much difference *inter se*. At first these were looked on as vagaries such as critics then expected from D, but when these cursives also bore them witness (partial though it might be) it was not so easy to dismiss them and a place was given to what before seemed mere freaks.

So in the Catholic Epistles we have 69, 214 and 216 forming a group which small though it be and divided as is sometimes their witness nevertheless gives us hope that we shall some day come across MSS. that will fill up here too the missing places if not as perfectly as we should like yet as well as we may reasonably expect. Thus to despise mixed MSS. because we cannot account for them or at present estimate their importance is to shut our own eyes. To accept or reject them just when and where it pleases is to deliberately blind ourselves. They have a value little as we can at present estimate it, and the work of Professor Lake on " Codex 1 and its allies " or of others on other groups or single MSS. is not lost labour. It but awaits a Darwin or a Herbert Spencer to co-ordinate them and their true value will be discovered.

Even by now we have learnt something of this. 200 years ago D was an insoluble puzzle and rather laughed at or at least dismissed as a freak. Then its Alexandrine element was discovered in its sympathy with B and L and it began to be tolerated. Then its affinity to certain Latin MSS. was seen and it became quite interesting, but still suspected, whilst later its close affinity to the Old Syriac has made men see that there is not a single reading but has its history, and that when the history of D is fully known we shall be very much nearer than at present to the original of the Greek Testament.

And so we conclude that though MSS. are mixed yet they may be inestimable treasures not to-day nor to-morrow but some day when we have found more missing links and can piece together the whole chain. We may never get nearer to the original than Eohippus is to the primitive ungulate, but even if we get thus far most of us would be satisfied, at least for the present.

The quotations from Φ and from 565 (Scrivener's 473, Tischendorf's 2^{pe}) are from Belsheim's edition kindly lent me by Professor Burkitt. The quotations from N, Σ and the cursive 700 are from the recent editions of their text.

Scrivener's "y" is often quoted as of great excellence. I have therefore inserted its readings fully in the tables. All these have been added in order to show the reader the value and use of the tables. It also brings them fairly up to date, and may save much useless labour. I regret that I have not as yet full and complete collations of 22 and 28.

The Western family is well represented in numbers, but not in variety. The readings of the Sinai Syriac have been inserted where extant and undoubted. I leave for the present to others the unravelling of the knots of relationship in this interesting family.

When we turn to the Versions we find an amount of mixture of all classes of readings that at first sight staggers us. The Greek MSS. except a few (mostly cursives) are easily divided into their families and seldom stray far, but in the Versions everything at first seems confusion. This however is really what we should expect, as the Versions are of course eclectic texts by their very nature, and we cannot expect the standard of selection to be at any rate the same as our

own. The easier and the more popular text would obviously be the favourite, and since the Western text was
certainly the best known in most cases we may expect to
find abundant traces of its influence. The Syrian text too
had been in existence long before many of the Versions
were made, and none of the later Versions are wholly
pre-Syrian in text. It is therefore necessary to divide
all the Versions by this latter test, and we then find
that the Old Syriac, the Old Latin and the Egyptian
Versions are alone predominately pre-Syrian together
with the " Jerusalem " Syriac.

The tables may well be left to tell their own tale
as regards the latter Versions. The Peshitta doubtless
belongs to the date assigned by Professor Burkitt, about
420 A.D. That date alone fits in with both the external
and internal evidence at our disposal. The date of the
Harklean is well known. It seems not improbable that
its present form differs from the original rather by
Western additions marked by asterisks than by actual
alterations of the text which was predominately Syrian
as indeed it still remains.

Of the Egyptian Versions all that can here be said
is that the Alexandrine text largely predominates in
both of them. I may also add that Tischendorf's
quotations are singularly accurate as tested by Mr
Horner's invaluable edition. The same accuracy indeed
characterises all Tischendorf's quotations from the other
Versions when tested by modern editions. Professor
Burkitt says, " It is only just to notice how excellent
is Tischendorf's report of syr-hl (text, mg.*) goth, arm,
aeth, also of the Egyptian versions—except for the fact
that there are now Sahidic and Fayyumic texts available, which were not known to Tischendorf." Such

witness will convince our readers that the quotations in the tables may be thoroughly relied upon.

The quotations from the Vulgate have been compared with Dr Wordsworth and White's edition in the few passages where the MSS. differ from the Clementine and altered when necessary. We are thus enabled to dispense with that mixture of first and second rate authorities that are here and there cited separately. This refers to the Holy Gospels and the Acts which have alone appeared so far. The very fact that we can at length refer to an authoritative edition and that one the ability of which no one can question, is a boon which no one can appreciate better than a student of textual criticism. Doubt, it is true, still remains in some comparatively few places, especially in the Acts, but not in any text cited in the tables. The close renderings of the Vulgate seldom leave much doubt as to the underlying Greek text. The reader will perhaps be surprised to see that in spite of revision its character is still essentially Western, but it was perhaps a wise caution that made St Jerome adopt a conservative course and not alter too much. We must remember too that the Western text all but held the entire field in his day and that the Syrian text, although seemingly known to him and used, was yet comparatively new. The likeness of his text to A, which is sometimes asserted, is seen to be far from true. In the Acts alone the Vulgate and A are both fundamentally Alexandrine. I have noticed but a few passages where distinctive A readings are adopted by St Jerome, but my search has not been so careful as perhaps might be wished.

A few remarks on the three primary groups may perhaps best be made at this point as it will afford an opportunity for placing several important Versions and Fathers in their relative positions instead of reviewing them one by one.

The great problem of New Testament criticism is undoubtedly the Western Text. Its origin is obscure, its classification doubtful, whilst its comparative value is altogether uncertain ; indeed there is scarcely a single point concerning it that is not the subject of debate and difficulty. It lies in the debateable land, and prejudice either in its favour or the reverse is fatal to any chance of ascertaining its right place or assigning to it a proper value.

Whilst its origin is wrapped in obscurity it is also wrapped in antiquity, and few or none of the early Fathers or Versions are free from its influence. The best and shortest account of the principal theories that have been so far held with regard to it is to be found in Professor Kirsopp Lake's admirable little book on " The Text of the New Testament" where a chapter is devoted to the subject. It must however not be forgotten that the question involves the higher criticism as well, and that textual criticism alone cannot be expected to solve it, though it may provide and arrange the material for such solution. Of this we may expect a further supply as soon as we get a complete edition of the Sahidic Gospels. Our hopes also lie in other directions, either in fresh discoveries of the works of early Syriac Fathers or in translations of these same Fathers in Armenian. Important finds have already been made, and these, we trust, are the earnest of others and still more important. At present it seems impossible to theorize with any prospect of success owing to this lack of material. We know something already, but our knowledge only goes

back to about 150 A.D., and much took place before
then, or at least may have done.

The classification of the authorities having a Western
text is fortunately an easier task. We have the Old
Syriac, the Old Latin, the Sahidic and the Jerusalem
Syriac amongst the Versions and Codex Bezae (D) of
the Greek MSS., besides many of the early Fathers.
When however we examine these in detail we find that
they fall into several groups and that little uniformity
prevails.

Of these groups by far the most important and
ancient is that formed by the Old Syriac and by
St Ephraem and St Cyprian, supported by *k*, *e*, *m* of
the Old Latin. To these we must perhaps add the
Sahidic and the Jerusalem Syriac, whilst D undoubtedly
contains more of this element than any other, especially
in St Luke, St John and the Acts. St Augustine also
belongs to it in a large measure, though in the Gospels
he often quotes the Vulgate. Tatian too belongs to
this group.

The next group, for want of a better name, may be
classed as European, and embraces *a b i* and *n* of the
Old Latin and the European Latin Fathers (except
Irenaeus). This group is not free from admixture with
the Syrian text (especially the Fathers) and thus is not
so important as the former.

Another group is formed by *g* and *q*, and consists
of Old Latin MSS. which have been very largely
admixed with the Syrian text. Their testimony is therefore diverse and their value doubtful, as far as criticism
is concerned. The Gothic and *f* (the Latin portion of
a Gotho-Latin MS.) ought to be included. This very
fact however shows that we cannot assign a later date than

350 A.D. to this group, a date which, it need scarcely be said, is earlier than any of our Greek MSS. except perhaps B.

The fourth group consists of Old Latin MSS. mixed with Vulgate, and embraces all the Old Latin authorities except those above mentioned. Of these *c* is much the best, and is practically half and half. Since the Vulgate has also a small Syrian element this group shows traces of the same.

It is impossible to attempt a closer classification of any of these groups, and general guidance alone can be given. For all practical purposes the last two groups may be entirely omitted since we have sufficient testimony to each of their component elements without their being called as witnesses. They are moreover without any early patristic support, and are only of service in determining the relationship of freshly discovered authorities.

When we come to discuss the value of the Western text as a whole it is extremely important that we should not be prejudiced by whatever we may have read, but examine for ourselves the evidence and form our own conclusions.

Western readings in common with all others divide themselves into three classes, namely additions, omissions and substitutions.

Of purely Western additions it must be confessed that they at once break down when tested by the rule of internal evidence, and only in a few cases where the patristic support is weighty do they merit much consideration. Many of them seem to be derived from traditional or apocryphal sources, and though possibly quite true in fact, were certainly not integral portions of the original.

Of Western alternative readings all we can say is that whilst often obviously wrong they must not be summarily dismissed without examination. Their age and their attestation alone demand this much, and as time goes on it is all but certain that more will be accepted as genuine than has hitherto been the case. A small proportion has every mark of excellence and has only been hitherto rejected owing to an undue prejudice in favour of the Alexandrine text.

Western *omissions* however occupy a very different position, and it is here that we meet with most difficulty in coming to a decision since internal evidence is so strongly in their favour. But we must not forget that even Western testimony is seldom unanimous and that the first two groups often differ in each case. Nor must we make too much of the fact of omission. The omissions made by St Matthew and St Luke in their narratives do not make the additional details found in St Mark doubtful. Another instance, kindly furnished me by Dr Joyce, occurs in the case of " The Testaments of the Twelve Patriarchs," a Jewish document with later Christian interpolations. In determining its text we are compelled chiefly to rely upon the original Greek and upon an Armenian version. Now the Christian insertions and alterations are far more numerous in the Greek, the original language of " The Testament," than in the version, and one would therefore be inclined to regard absence from the Armenian as a decisive test, but Dr Charles, in his edition, says that " on almost every page he (the Armenian translator) is guilty of unjustifiable omissions." So that absence in this case is far from a certain test. We have an extreme instance of a similar state of affairs in the case of the Ignatian

Epistles where critics encounter three different recensions. Of these the longest is universally rejected, the second is all but universally received, whilst the third and shortest is universally rejected too. Some of the most important Western omissions can be explained on doctrinal grounds, and the doubt remains in all cases as to whether a text which adds so much as the Western would not with very little reason reject wherever it thought right. We must not judge early ages by our own day, nor compare their canons of reverence for the words of Holy Scripture with the days of plenary inspiration. Their faith was not in a text but in a Person, and there was no counting of every jot and tittle of the New Law, whatever may have been the case with the Old. Very few accept the additions or omissions of the Septuagint, however interesting the question as to their origin. On the whole the Western text gives us the link between the New Testament and the Christian Apocrypha and is the first trace of that tendency to supplement the simple words of the New Testament that is afterwards found so marvellously developed in later Christian literature. It is not however the less interesting on that account, and we must not imagine it to be unorthodox or schismatical. It is as Catholic as the Logia, and no argument can get over the fact that whether rightly or wrongly it was used as genuine by those to whose opinions we defer in other matters. At the same time we must not forget that Origen who lived so much nearer than we do, and Jerome who lived later but made use of the oldest authorities procurable, alike reject both Western additions and omissions, though accepting not a few of the other Western readings. This is an objective historic fact which, accept at whatever value we may, seems to discount what after all are decisions based merely on the rules of internal evidence.

To go further is to show prejudice. To say less is to hide from ourselves the real facts of the case. To reject anything Western simply because it is Western is neither reason nor criticism.

It is necessary to add that even those Fathers who are most Western differ very much from the Versions that are our main authority for a Western Text. Close for instance as is the agreement between St Cyprian and *k*, the number of times when the latter and its fellows stand absolutely without any patristic support is enormous. This is doubtless owing largely to the meagre amount of early patristic attestation, but cannot be entirely due to this. A continuous Western commentary on the Gospels is what we should have liked. Our only continuous Western commentaries are "Ambrosiaster" on the Pauline Epistles, Victorinus on the Philippians and Andreas on the Apocalypse. A comparison between the quotations of the Western Fathers and the Western Versions as given in the tables will show that the former often exercised much discretion in their rejection or acceptance of readings and knew of other texts besides the Western. Moreover when they make express quotations from particular Gospels or refer to old authorities their testimony is most frequently to an Alexandrine text, just as we commonly quote from the Authorized Version, but where it better suits our purpose refer to the Revised.

The Syrian text merits attention if only from the fact that all but about one per cent. of our authorities are pure Syrian. A few remarks on its origin, its characteristics, and its value will therefore not be out of place.

In tracing its origin it is best to begin at the sixth century, when there can be no doubt it was fully established, and to work backwards.

The fifth century gives us A, C and the Peshitta. Of these A, the later, is most Syrian in character, whilst C is least so, the Peshitta lying about midway. The struggle for supremacy had not yet issued in total victory.

In the fourth century we find St Chrysostom has seemingly accepted the Syrian text, but not entirely, as only 60 per cent. of his quotations are pure Syrian. The Gothic, a little earlier still, shows a very similar state of things. Following the Fathers we have Basil with about 30 per cent. of Syrian readings, and Eusebius with about 25. This is too great a proportion to be accidental, and I think there can be no doubt that the Syrian text existed, but was comparatively recent. Eusebius and Basil it will be remembered both belong to Caesarea.

The trail then thins out, or rather is all but lost, for the quotations of Methodius are insufficient in number for our purpose and Hippolytus is seemingly mainly Western.

When however we come to Origen we have again a plenteous store of quotations, and on analysing them we find that he has only about eight per cent. of Syrian readings, so that the probability in this case is that the Syrian here borrowed from Origen and not *vice-versa*. The Syrian text may therefore with much probability be placed somewhere in the latter half of the third century. It is interesting to note that ℵᶜ of the seventh century tells us that the text has been compared with a MS. belonging to Pamphilus (fl. 294 A.D.). Now the text of

ℵᶜ is all but pure Syrian both in the Gospels and in St Paul's Epistles. Pamphilus as we know was the apologist of Origen and the friend of Eusebius. If then Pamphilus had anything to do with a text nothing is more probable than that he should take at least eight per cent. of his readings from Origen and that Eusebius should accept his edition as authoritative. Further we dare not go.

The characteristics of the Syrian text are exactly those we should expect from a revised text. It is in short a full text, and neglects the omissions of both the Alexandrine and the Western text, filling up the latter from the former and *vice-versa* and sometimes uniting both. It also corrects the Greek of the older texts, giving us for instance a singular verb after a neuter plural and adding the article where seemingly needed, besides often changing the tenses or order of words where such seemed called for. The particles too are frequently changed, and in short every endeavour has been made to polish up or soften down the simple ruggedness of the more ancient texts.

But this is not all. The Syrian text is in the true sense of the word eclectic, and adopts whatever ancient reading it found that seemed most suitable. Especially in not a few cases it adopts the readings of the Old Syriac, and is sometimes the only additional evidence that we have of the existence of such readings.

All this has a bearing on its value, and we are obliged to admit that for a reading to be Syrian it is not necessary for it to be late. In fact we cannot doubt that as we obtain further ancient testimony we shall be able to carry back many Syrian readings to a much earlier period.

This should make us pause before rejecting any Syrian reading that is not easily accounted for and that has the support of internal evidence. It may be the remnant of a very ancient text and not an amendment. Even if we place the Syrian text some time before 300 A.D., it is nearly a hundred years older than our earliest Greek MS.

At the same time it must not be overlooked that in no case where the Syrian text is called in to be a kind of make-weight or arbiter can we get away from the original uncertainty, and on the whole we must put aside the Syrian text as rather adding to our uncertainty than removing it. It was an honest attempt to stay the corruption of the text of the New Testament, and we cannot be too thankful that it was undertaken so early and provided the Church with an authorized version. It was a success too, and deserved to succeed if only from its motive. It has been fortunately handed down to us in such a pure form that one of the easiest tasks of the textual critic is to separate Syrian from non-Syrian. It has served its generation and served it admirably. To discuss it on the principle of giving a dog a bad name and hanging it is to be unjust to it. Its editor as much merits our approbation as St Jerome does for his Vulgate or Origen for his Septuagint.

As regards the Alexandrine text the really important question is whether it is a recension at all and not a direct descendant from the original. And this is extremely difficult to decide owing to lack both of material and of historic evidence.

It is necessary to remind the reader that every transcript has not only errors of its own, but also those of its ancestors, and that moreover an interval of about

300 years separates our earliest Greek MS. from the original. Thus there can be little doubt that no MS. we now have is a direct transcript from the original.

If the Alexandrine authorities are examined we find that B, our earliest, is remarkably free from clerical errors and seemingly also from incorrect readings, as the contemporary hand has made very few alterations. On turning to ℵ, which cannot be placed later than the first quarter of the fifth century, and probably belongs to the fourth century also, we find clerical errors in abundance as well as numerous contemporary corrections. The difference between these two MSS. is probably due to the ancestors in the first case being few whilst in the second they are comparatively numerous. Of the other Alexandrine MSS. the same is true in varying degrees, as we might expect from their later date. The point to be noticed is that the variation of the Alexandrine authorities *inter se* is often very great. The Syrian MSS. e.g. agree very closely with each other after the fifth century. When however we come to compare ℵ and B we find so much variation that Dr Burgon was nearer the mark than usual when he said that it was easier to find where they differed than where they agreed. This would seem to prove that whilst we use the word Alexandrine as a convenient term for describing them collectively, yet in reality they are not the result of a revision in the true sense of the word, but rather descendants each in its own line from the original.

And yet such texts may have been connected with Alexandria in the main, since we know that there alone existed that reverence for the *ipsissima verba* that is wanting elsewhere. It was here therefore that each would best preserve its own idiosyncrasies instead of being made to follow a common model.

And these idiosyncrasies are a real puzzle. Internal evidence tells us to accept the more difficult reading, and no other rule works well or is so universally held to be essential. And it is when this canon is applied that Syrian and Western readings are so frequently condemned as emendations. And yet it may be that we are sometimes accepting real clerical errors and blunders of the scribes rather than the true text.

It is upon this point that Dean Burgon seizes and picks out about two or three dozen readings, some of which one feels are really blunders. Upon these he (and Scrivener) ring the changes and take them as true specimens of the Alexandrine text instead of as quite exceptional. No one too can read Dr Hort's Appendix without feeling that there is much special pleading in many of these cases, and that it would have been often much better to accept the difficulty rather than justify the reading. The number of such passages is so small that the great preeminence of the Alexandrine family in general would not have been impaired, and the real state of the case would have been better represented. And even though the canon would have been infringed, yet in these cases *exceptio probat regulam*, and surely even canons must have their limit of application just as everything else human. This it will be said makes internal evidence the ultimate criterion. Not so, for in nearly all cases we have Alexandrine evidence too for another reading, but since this has often the support of the Western text, it is hastily rejected as Western. The difficulty is, of course, to choose from the two alternatives, but surely reason and sense have something to do with the matter, and no law can be accepted as infallible in such a case. This canon and others have to do with the probabilities of transcription, and are performing their function only when such cases arise. But again we must repeat that the important point to note is that the very preservation of these blunders shows that this class of text preferred to preserve rather than to amend, and in fact increases our confidence in their absolute fidelity. An untouched portrait is after all more true to nature than the usual product of the studio. It must be confessed it is not always as flattering. Thus one is strongly inclined to think our Alexandrine MSS. underwent no revision but on the contrary are careful transcripts of their exemplars. A similar case is of course to be found in the Hebrew text of the Old Testament where error is perpetuated rather than resort to conjecture or emendation.

Another point must be touched upon, however slightly. If a careful survey of the tables of the Gospels be made it will be found how much less Western the Nicene and ante-Nicene Fathers are than the Versions. It is impossible to bring out this point sufficiently clearly in the tables owing to the paucity of quotations from some of the Fathers, but a good general idea can be obtained, and that idea is not unfavourable to the Alexandrine text, and if a table be drawn up of express citations by the Fathers the result is the same. Thus it would not be right to say that the early Fathers have a *pure* Western text. They bear unequivocal witness to the existence of such a text in their day, but they bear as clear a witness to the Alexandrine, and when actual variations are noticed the Western reading is not favoured in more than ten per cent. of cases at the most.

When we turn from the Gospels to the Pauline Epistles, where citations are more numerous, the same thing is found as regards these Fathers. It all seems to show that the Fathers knew that the text was corrupt and used it with caution, especially where, as in St Paul's Epistles, exactness was essential. All this is vague enough, I know, but the tables will give a good general idea of the real state of the case and assure us that there was no real revision at Alexandria but that in that place the text was handed down more faithfully (errors included) than elsewhere. A revision would have fallen into the trap and given us false but plausible readings. The Alexandrine avoids the snare and must ever be our purest and best authority for the New Testament. Like the sun it may have spots, but who finds fault with the sun on that account, or how much do they interfere with its light and heat? So this text has its faults, *humanum est errare,* but we may add, "even its failings lean to virtue's side," and are the best proofs of its general faithfulness.

There is little doubt that as time goes on and knowledge of relationship increases, we shall advance to more scientific methods, and that an attempt will be made to give a numerical value to our authorities. In such a case triple readings will be invaluable and enable us to reduce them all to a common denominator. Percentages will obviously be the best.

For instance we have the following for the Vulgate[1]:

|                    |     | Readings | Percentage |
|--------------------|-----|----------|------------|
| Western readings   | . . . | 52     | 46·44      |
| Alexandrine „      | . . . | 28     | 25·00      |
| Syrian „           | . . . | 32     | 28·57      |

[1] This is only an instance and is worked out to the second decimal point as an example, not with any idea that the result is reliable to such an extent.

Such tables of percentages when worked out for Fathers and Versions must ultimately lead to more intimate knowledge of sub-groups. The next step will be the recognition of the fact that groups are not of the value indicated by the sum of their (say, Alexandrine) elements, but by their products. Hence a small group may have an exceedingly high value. With this second stage we have at present nothing to do. Knowledge of documents is our aim. Their comparative value comes afterwards.

It must not be hidden from the reader that in these divisions into families the lesser divisions must perforce be ignored. The Western family has several sub-groups. The Alexandrine may perhaps be divided into two, Westcott and Hort's "Neutral" and the so-called "Alexandrine," though to my mind such division seems not at present warranted. Our classification does not go at present so far. Some years ago zoologists were divided into "lumpers" and "splitters." The one ignored lesser divisions, the other insisted upon them as essential to classification. The latter amongst textual critics may find much to assist them in our tables, although only the groups themselves are given. This is because the sub-groups are usually distinguished by special mixture from other families rather than by peculiar readings. This is an important point to remember. A sub-group is not usually an entirely new breed, but a cross-breed, with all the vigour oftentimes of the cross-breed (e.g. the early Syriac text and the early African), but still not totally *sui generis*. As to the origin of the various groups little need be said, as this too belongs to a much later stage. A number of those readings that Westcott and Hort call "Alexandrine" are, it seems to me, essentially Western, and come from that great centre of early Christian activity where the Western text seems to have originated—I mean of course Syria.

The paucity of the Patristic citations, especially in St Mark, will probably astonish most of those that are not familiar with the subject. The reader should study the quotations from all four Gospels where the citations from one Gospel alone are not sufficient to ascertain the character of a Father's text. This is absolutely necessary in the case of e.g. Augustine and others if we want to ascertain, say, the text current in Africa or to solve similar problems.

# THE ACTS AND CATHOLIC EPISTLES

Although the Gospels and the Acts differ in detail and in extent of attestation yet the great three families are still plainly to be discerned and hence easily separated. Not to multiply needless comment of what the tables make quite evident we may say that the only real difficulty lies in the want of a little more pure Western attestation.

In the Gospels we had the Old Latin, the Old Syrian, and D, besides others more or less pure, whilst in the Acts it shrinks to D as our only pure text. Not that there is in reality any difficulty. The characteristics of D are the same as before, and there can be no more doubt as to its origin than when we find say a single Lascar in Liverpool or a " Nigger " in the Strand.

The text of E (and therefore of the Venerable Bede) is, it will be noticed, not so Western in character as is sometimes represented, and cannot alone be used as a sure indicator of Western readings. The quotations from the Fathers fortunately become so numerous and distinctive as to afford fairly good evidence both for time and place of text. They do not seem to vary much from corresponding quotations in the Gospels.

The long array of cursives quoted at the bottom are of little use. We find in 137 a largely Western document. For many of its readings I am greatly indebted to the kindness of the Rev. A.V. Valentine Richards, M.A., of Christ's College, who is now engaged in editing its text. The Western readings in "c Scrivener" are also fairly numerous. In the Catholic Epistles we are without the assistance of D, and thus have no approximately pure Western guide. Scrivener "a" (and its brother 69) are perhaps the best, but the Western element in them seems to cease altogether after 1 John. The same applies to Scrivener's "c," which in the Catholic Epistles is fairly closely related to "a." The Harklean too is largely Western.

It may be pointed out that the remarks in Scrivener (Vol. I. p. 300) to Acts 221 are far from correct. I quote them as a specimen of similar careless statements that abound, particularly in the last edition. "This copy (i.e. Acts 221) is full of instructive variations, being nearest akin to the Harklean Syriac *cum asterisco* and to $c^{scr}$ (184), then to $a^{scr}$ (182), 137, 100, 66**, 69, $d^{scr}$ (185), next to 27, 29, 57**." All we can say is that 221 must be a prodigy to be akin to MSS. as diverse as these. On page 298 we are told that Scrivener's "c" much resembles 61 (our Scrivener's "o"), a statement the recklessness of which is only equalled by its ignorance. It will not surprise us to find on page 289 that the editor (Mr Miller) himself tells us that 61 "is much overrated." Before going through the Catholic Epistles a special preliminary investigation was made of pure Western readings for guides to identification, and there can be no doubt that B alone of the primary uncials is all but free. I have not ventured to take any reading of B alone as Alexandrine when opposed to the other two (or three) primary uncials. Such a course seemed safer, and only meant the rejection of the very few places where this occurs. The fact that in all cases the Syrian and Alexandrine readings are so well attested makes the identification of the small residue as Western the more unmistakable.

If there had been a large remnant (both non-Syrian and non-Alexandrine), and if the conflict of authorities had been great, the case would be far otherwise. Under any circumstances what we most want in the Catholic Epistles is a pure Western Greek text to assist the identification.

The similarity between 15 and 18 will be noticed. Other similar parallels occur, and many other remarks might be made, but careful study of the table will render most of them unnecessary, and to draw parallels on insufficient evidence has always been the besetting sin of textual critics.

The text of Acts 36 and the quotations from "Catena" (Cramer's) have been altogether ignored, as in most cases they will be found quoted again under the headings of the respective Fathers.

# THE PAULINE EPISTLES

Here again there is little difficulty, the three families being well represented by comparatively pure members, the Western being especially easy to detect in these Epistles owing to our having D (and its copy E) and F (and its brother G), the two last agreeing in all the passages cited in the table.

The only non-homogeneous MS. is 17, which is all but pure Syrian in Romans and all but pure Alexandrine elsewhere. It is a text of quite primary importance, as is the second hand of 67.

Except D and F the Vulgate has far the largest Western element. There is too a small Western element in B, which however does not show itself in any triple readings as far as my observation goes. The combinations BD and BF are however by no means to be always condemned off hand.

The cursives show particularly pure Syrian texts. 73 seems to contain a fairly large Western element in the latter portion, Scrivener's remark (Vol. I. p. 290, sub Acts 68) that "In the text of St Paul it much resembles Paul 17" being far from correct.

The long list of Fathers will at last enable the reader to compare the text shown in various places and at various times. The East, the West, Egypt, Africa,

Italy (and North Italy especially), Alexandria, Asia and Byzantium all find witnesses. It needs no skill to draw inferences. We draw attention to the important Western text presented by "Ambrosiaster." Comparison between it and D or F will show what vigour the Western text had and how much Jerome's work (at that time perhaps going on) was needed. No wonder too that Jerome left so much of the Old Latin unrevised. A perfect revision would not have had a ghost of a chance of reception in either Italy or Europe. (Cf. the R.V. in our own country.)

# THE TEXT OF THE APOCALYPSE

The text of the Apocalypse has for a long time been
looked upon as an all but insoluble puzzle. We propose
therefore to discuss it at some length, and to show how
things fall into their place when subjected to the same
process of analysis as the remainder of the New Testament.

The first thing to do is to make a careful preliminary
survey of all the triple readings. These are at any rate
quite sufficient for us to grasp the real bearing of the
evidence. In doing this we are obliged to read the
whole *apparatus criticus* in Tischendorf, and in so doing
we find the evidence of triple readings fully confirmed
in every point.

We first discover a very large group which comprises
B₂ only amongst the uncials, about 30 of the cursives,
and Arethas only amongst the Fathers. The text of
Andreas in Codex Coislinianus has been altered to
conform particularly to this group. The absence of
attestation from the Versions (except here and there a
quotation) and the all but entire absence of the Fathers
enable us to identify this group without much chance of
error as the Syrian text.

The next group that strikes us is one that includes P
(to a large extent) and nearly twenty of the cursives

(amongst them being the parent of our Textus Receptus) and Andreas amongst the Fathers. This family has a fair amount of support amongst the Versions, though none are unmixed adherents. Amongst the Fathers too we find traces of it, especially in Primasius and the Latins. Primasius does not wholly adhere to it, but the difference can easily be explained. His text when fully examined is seen to be identical with that of St Cyprian. Now the latter as we know uses in the Gospels a text all but identical with *k* (Codex Bobiensis) which is an African text. We have but to suppose that his text in the Apocalypse was of the same family, and every reading is accounted for. Primasius it is true lived long after St Cyprian, but Hadrumetum, his see, is but a stone's throw comparatively from Carthage, and hence there is no violence in the supposition that their texts were similar—how similar our table at once shows. Andreas of Caesarea lived in the sixth century, but he also lived not far from where at any rate the Western text once flourished, as seen in the Old Syriac. The differences between Andreas and Primasius are not any greater than the differences between the Old Syriac and the Old Latin. No less than seven of the cursives on our list contain the commentary of Andreas (amongst them, as we have seen, the MS. which forms the basis of our Textus Receptus) and of the first 100 cursives in Scrivener's list, which alone were known in Tischendorf's time, the following contain the comments of Andreas: 1, 18, 21, 35, 41 (extracts), 49, 62, 63, 67, 72, 73, 79, 80, 81, and perhaps others that we have not been able to trace. "Andreas-cois" is numbered 121 in Dr Gregory's list. We have placed AN against such as occur in the tables for facility of reference. The texts accompanied by the commentary of Arethas are 4, 10 (scholia), 64, 68, 77, and 95 (epitome). Those in our list are marked AR. Number 6 contains a catena seemingly from Arethas, and the following have some commentary of which the source is unknown to the writer, 59, 74, and 85. We cannot then fail to identify P and the Andreas text with the great Western family. Its general agreement with Primasius, Cyprian, Victorinus and others is too close for any other conclusion.

There now remains a small but consistent band which forms a group of itself. A is all but free from mixture, as is C, and to a less extent ℵ, whilst not one of the cursives in our list is a member of this small family. It is however well supported by the Versions, though not entirely so, and the early Fathers bear all but constant witness to it.

On account of the importance of the Western text we have given a separate table of practically every Western reading where a difference of word occurs. In this table a cross denotes an Alexandrine reading afterwards adopted by the Syrian revision. The dash indicates a pure Western reading. We have omitted readings in which the article alone is involved as not necessary to our purpose. Differences of order too have been omitted if unimportant.

In every MS., Version and Father, we find more or less errors of homoioteleuton in the text of the Apocalypse. This is due to the short clauses which are its characteristic, and to their similarity of ending. It is far the most frequent of all errors in all authorities, and often causes serious doubt. It may be added that ℵ seems to have been written with more care than usual though not entirely free from signs of haste.

It will be seen that the Andreas text has been the predominant factor in producing mixture, and that few of our authorities are free from its influence. It forms in fact the key to the solution of the problem of the Apocalyptic text. It seems also to prove the excellency of the method here adopted. To leave Andreas out of our calculations is indeed to play Hamlet without the ghost.

Our present experience leaves perhaps little hope that much can be expected from extensive collation of cursives. But the smallness of the Alexandrine group makes it imperative that something should be done. Valuable texts must surely be hidden somewhere, and how invaluable even one more purely Alexandrine text would be no one can estimate. A preliminary survey on the lines laid down would soon discover such treasures. Is it too much to hope for? Not that the text of the Apocalypse is at all in a bad state. The really doubtful places are few and unimportant, but still we cannot leave it until some at least are cleared up. The Word of God demands as a right that something should be done. At present books are written on problems which can never be satisfactorily solved until more evidence is obtained. We want not hypotheses but data. We have the former. The latter lie at hand, but unregarded.

# EXCURSUS ON THE FERRAR GROUP

In my notes on the Gospels I referred at some length to the question of mixed MSS. and illustrated my remarks by discussing the relationship of Codex 1 and its allies, passing over the Ferrar group as less interesting owing to the much larger amount of agreement between its various members.

It is probable however that most of my readers know more about the Ferrar group than about any other, so that I have decided to discuss the mutual relationship of the members, so far as the material at my disposal will allow. The more important question of the relationship of the group to the primary families must, I fear, be left out for the present.

The Ferrar group consists of about ten MSS. all of them of the twelfth century or later and all of them except one (69) written in South Italy. This seemingly purely local text cannot be later than about 1000 A.D. and may be much earlier.

The MSS. of this group so far known are 13, 69, 124, 346, 543, 788, 826, 828, 983 and another in a monastery near Serres called by Prof. von Soden ε 1054. Besides these we have (according to the Professor) two allied

MSS. 174 and 837. The Professor says that 543 and 826 are very closely connected, as are 13 and 346.

Of these MSS. I can here discuss only the first five, as I have no collations of any of the remainder.

The material for the discussion consists not of the readings given in the Appendix of this work but is taken from my list of pure Syrian readings to which reference has been made at the beginning of the notes on the Gospels. Owing to lacunae in one or other of the MSS. the readings available (i.e. where all five MSS. are extant) are 141, but it must be remembered that all these readings are important and not mere cases of differences of particles, or tenses and the like.

When we come to the tabulation of these we are obliged to adopt the following classification. S will indicate a pure Syrian reading. A indicates a non-Syrian reading, that is, one supported by the Alexandrine and Western authorities. This group I prefer to call non-Syrian rather than use the question-begging term pre-Syrian, though such readings are undoubtedly both. P signifies as always a reading peculiar to the whole group or to one or more members of it.

We can now tabulate the readings as follows:

|  | S | A | P |
|---|---|---|---|
| Common to all | 82 | 16 | 4 |

or 72 per cent., showing a very close relationship between all the members.

|  | S | A |
|---|---|---|
| Common to 13, 69, 124 | 1 | 1 |
|     „    13, 69, 346 | 12 | 7 |
|     „    13, 124, 346 | 5 | 2 |
|     „    69, 124, 346 | 0 | 0 |

Here we may neglect the first as too insignificant to affect the final result. The last of course cannot be tabulated. Thus the grandparents of the five MSS. were only two in number as far as our knowledge goes. 543 is left out entirely for a reason that will appear presently.

The next generation gives us:

|  | | S | A | P |
|---|---|---|---|---|
| Common to 13, 69 | | 0 | 5 | 0 |
| „ | 13, 124 | 0 | 0 | 0 |
| „ | 13, 346 | 0 | 1 | 0 |
| „ | 69, 124 | 1 | 2 | 0 |
| „ | 69, 346 | 0 | 0 | 0 |
| „ | 124, 346 | 6 | 0 | 0 |

Of these only the first and last need to be considered as of any importance. 543 is again left out.

We now come to the MSS. themselves and find:

|  | | S | A | P |
|---|---|---|---|---|
| Peculiar to | 13 | 0 | 0 | 0 |
| „ | 69 | 0 | 5 | 1 |
| „ | 124 | 6 | 13 | 0 |
| „ | 346 | 1 | 1 | 0 |
| „ | 543 | 0 | 0 | 0 |

From this it is obvious that 13 and 543 are closely related, as in every one of the 141 readings they are alike. They are probably therefore copies of the same exemplar. Hence we have in the other tables given only 13, and the reader must bear in mind that 543 is a mere duplicate. 346 too, according to the above, has little or no independence.

It is unnecessary for me to construct the genealogy step by step, as an example has already been given of

the process.  The result therefore will alone be given.
Here it is :

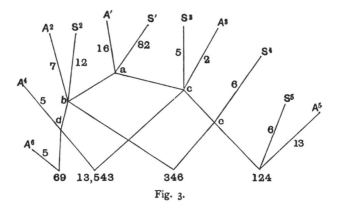

Fig. 3.

It must be confessed that it looks rather like "the
fretful porcupine," but if studied it may give us more
information than we think if we judge only by the looks.

The first inference we may draw is that to reconstruct
the archetype we may leave 13, 543, and 346 entirely
out of the question.  They have nothing in them that
cannot be found in 69 and 124, which latter are quite
independent for at least three generations.

Now taking these two MSS. separately we see in the
case of 124 three successive waves of Syrian corruption
(S³, S⁴, S⁵) whilst in the case of 69 we have only one
wave (S²).  The reader must not imagine that the waves
A² and S², or A³ and S³ etc., were strictly contemporane-
ous.  Such is by no means likely to have been the case
and is only the result of our loss of intermediate links.
Had 13, 543 and 346 been more independent we might
have known much more.  As it is we must leave matters
until more collations are in our possession.

The real puzzle of the genealogy is to account for the successive non-Syrian waves ($A^2$, $A^3$, $A^4$, $A^5$, $A^6$). Nor shall I attempt to pretend that I can solve it off-hand. Its solution really lies in one or more unknown members of the group that were obviously more pure than any of the above five. I am inclined to think that many of the Syrian readings in the ancestry of 124 are due to some lacunae caused by mutilation in one of its progenitors, as the Syrian readings peculiar to this MS. come in two or three patches instead of being evenly distributed throughout the text. But hypotheses are usually only excuses for ignorance, and textual criticism has too often been like a building erected with untempered mortar. For my own part I confess I cannot make bricks without straw.

NOTES ON SELECTED PASSAGES
BY PROFESSOR F. C. BURKITT

# INTRODUCTION TO PROF. BURKITT'S
# NOTES ON SELECT PASSAGES

In a letter to Professor Burkitt a statement was made by the author to the effect that the Syrian text had borrowed various readings from a large number of sources, and the following case was given. More than twenty years ago I made a collection of pure Syrian readings throughout the New Testament. These were arranged in three classes according to importance. Class A in St Mark's Gospel comprised 43 examples of the most important. In 1892 Mrs Lewis discovered the Sinaitic Codex of the Old Syriac Version, and in due course a translation was published in 1894. It was then found that of the 43 readings in my Class A in St Mark (where the Curetonian Syriac is wanting for all but a few verses at the end) nine at least (i.e. 20 per cent.) had the support of the new Sinaitic Codex and had to be discarded from the tables.

All this was mentioned to Professor Burkitt, and in reply he requested me to give him instances. As far as I was able from notes in my Tischendorf this was done, and in due course forwarded to him, and it was in reply that the following notes on each passage were sent, together with permission to add them to this work.

How much this enhances the value of this work I fully appreciate, as will the reader who knows anything of the subject.

Professor Burkitt's notes are given direct from his own MS., and no comments of my own are added, as the whole question will be discussed when the pure Syrian readings come under review. In the seventh instance I was misled by the translation used which (excellent as it is) here seemingly slipped. I need not say that it was not Professor Burkitt's own translation.

In answer to the question "What special conclusion do you draw?" I can only say that these instances and others confirm the general conclusion that the Syrian text is in the true sense of the word eclectic, drawing "Various readings" of various value from various sources. Oftentimes it picked up a diamond, and sometimes a bit of broken glass, sometimes it rescued a bit of gold from all but oblivion, and sometimes it gives us brass or lacquer without distinction from the nobler metal. It was for all the world like a magpie, and the result is not unlike a magpie's nest.

The remainder of Professor Burkitt's notes will be discussed all being well when the last part of this work appears. They refer to subjects which lie at the foundation where mists are thick and light but scanty, and where indeed pure textual criticism comes in contact with the higher with much the same result we might expect when the objective and subjective meet.

# NOTE UPON SOME AGREEMENTS BETWEEN THE SINAI PALIMPSEST AND THE *TEXTUS RECEPTUS* IN ST MARK'S GOSPEL

The following agreements have been noticed between the Sinai Palimpsest of the Old Syriac Version (syr.*S*) and the *Textus Receptus* (ς) against the "better authorities" (אBD lat. vt &c)[1]:

1. Mk v 3 οὐκέτι οὐδεὶσ אBC*DLΔ 13 &c 28 565 *b c e f ff* vg arm

   οὐδεὶσ ἔτι 1 &c

   οὐδεὶσ (alone) ς *i q r* syr.*S* -vg-hkl aeth boh sah goth

   [The really noteworthy feature here is that arm supports οὐκέτι. Otherwise the omission of the word would have been put down to a mere simplification of redundant negatives, the true text having οὐδὲ...οὐκέτι οὐδεὶσ.... With regard to the question whether the omission of οὐκέτι in ς and its non-representation in syr.*S* are really connected, it may be noticed that syr.*S*

[1] In what follows ς is to be regarded as a symbol for "'Stephanus (Ed. 3) and all known Greek MSS. not otherwise specified."

entirely simplifies the construction of the Greek ("and there was not anyone able with chains[1] to bind him") the Peshitta does follow the Greek order ("and with chains no one was able to bind him"). The Harclean Syriac faithfully gives a rendering of οὐδὲ before ἁλύσεσιν, where syr.*S* and the Peshitta have a simple "and."

Thus the evidence tends to suggest that syr.*S* really represents a Greek text which omitted οὐκέτι, but we cannot be certain that it does.]

2. Mk vii 5 (after the parenthesis about Jewish customs)

καὶ ἐπερωτῶσιν ℵBDL 1 &c 33 565 700
latt (exc. *f*) syr.vg aeth boh
ἔπειτα ἐπερωτ. ς *f* syr.*S* -hkl arm goth

[syr.*S* has "and after these things," syr.hkl has "afterwards," so that the reading of syr.hkl is not a survival of the Old Syriac, but the result of revision from the Greek. It is not improbable that the reading of syr.*S* is really a rendering of ἔπειτα (see 1 Cor. xv 7ª syr.vg); at the same time this phrase or an equivalent is actually used in Matt. ii 13 *S C*, Matt. xi 7 *S*, Lk. xx 20 *S C*, as a kind of translator's bridge by way of colourless paraphrase, where the Greek for some reason is slurred over[2]: it should not be forgotten that syr.*S* in Mk vii 4 abridges the catalogue at "pots," omitting "brazen vessels" with or without "beds." N.B. The irrational paragraph-division of syr.*S* in Mk vii 13 suggests that one of the ancestors of syr.*S* (probably the Diatessaron) had the Western or Syrian interpolation to Mk vii 8 : see Diat^ar xx 26.]

---

[1] Or, "with a chain" (=BC*L 565 *c e*): the plural points are, as a matter of fact, illegible in syr.*S*.

[2] I do not add Matt. viii 5, because the Latins have *post haec autem*. In Diat^ar xxiv 30 (=Lk. ix 38ª) the story is introduced by "and after this."

3. Mk vii 14 πάλιν אBDLΔ latt (exc. *f*, *c*) syr.hl.mg
   boh aeth
   πάντα ς *f* syr.*S* [-vg]- hl.txt arm goth
   om. 565 al² *c*

[Note that syr.vg inserts Ἰησοῦσ (= Γ) and puts πάντα in a different place from syr.*S*. Both here and in vii 5 we feel the loss of the African Latin, neither *e* nor *k* being extant.]

4. Mk viii 29 καὶ αὐτὸσ ἐπηρώτα αὐτούσ ⎫
         אBC\*LΔ *q* boh syr^pal (vid) ⎪
       αὐτὸσ δὲ ἐπηρώτα αὐτούσ D 565 ⎬ ...(i)
        *a ff* sah ⎭

   λέγει αὐτοῖσ 1 &c 28 syr.*S* arm ⎫
       aeth (fay¹) ⎬ ...(ii)
   "saith to them Jesus" syr.vg ⎭

   καὶ αὐτὸσ λέγει αὐτοῖσ ς syr.hl goth ...(iii)
   *tunc dicit illis b i* vg (also *r* with ⎫
       *ihs* after *illis*) ⎬
   *tunc dicit discipulis suis f* ⎭
   *ipsos autem interrogauit dicens c*
   om. *k* (the *late* corrector of *k* adds *et ait i*[*p*]*se*)

[Thus ς and syr.*S* do not here agree: ς appears to be a conflation of (ii), an "Eastern" text, with (i). (i) was also found in the West, but an early Western text omitted the clause (so *k*), and the loss was made up in various ways (so *c*, *b f i r* vg).]

5. Mk ix 17 ἀπεκρίθη αὐτῷ אBDLΔ 28 33 *a b*(*c*)(*i*)*k q*
   boh
   ἀποκριθεὶσ...εἶπεν ς (1 &c) (13 &c) (565) *f* vg
   syr.*S* -vg arm

---

¹ I.e. the Fayyumic, or Middle Egyptian text. I cannot remember whence I got this.

(*c i* add *dicens*, 1 &c 13 &c 565 add αὐτῷ, and
1 &c 13 &c read ἐκ τοῦ ὄχλου εἰσ.)

[The literary tendency of syr.vt is to substitute plain
" said " or "saith" for "answered" or "answered and said."
I cannot doubt therefore that syr.*S* supports ἀποκριθεὶσ...
εἶπεν here. It is strange in that case that it does not
add αὐτῷ with its usual allies 1 &c 13 &c 565.]

    6*a*.  Mk ix 31 μετὰ τρεῖσ ἡμέρασ ℵBCDLΔ lat.vt
        (exc. *f* ) syr.hl.mg boh

        τῇ τρίτῃ ἡμέρᾳ ς *f*-vg syr.*S* -vg-hl.txt arm
        aeth goth

    6*b*.  Mk x 34 (same division of authorities)

[The early Syriac texts are so much given to har-
monisation, that it would be plausible here to refer
simply to the parallels in Matthew and Luke as the
source of the Syriac rendering. But the Latin variations
suggest that all the occurrences of μετὰ τρεῖσ ἡμέρασ
and τῇ τρίτῃ ἡμέρᾳ should be considered together. The
net result will be to confirm μετὰ τρεῖσ ἡμέρασ for Mark
and τῇ τρίτῃ ἡμέρᾳ for Luke (τῇ ἡμέρᾳ τῇ τρίτῃ Lk. xviii
33)[1]. But while τῇ τρίτῃ ἡμέρᾳ is assured in Matt. xx 19,
μετὰ τρεῖσ ἡμέρασ is read by D lat.vt in xvi 21 (hiat
syr.*S*) and by D lat.vt syr.*S* in xvii 23 : it seems to me
not unlikely this is the true text of Matthew.

In Mk 1 &c 13 &c 565 syrr consistently attest τῇ τρίτῃ
ἡμέρᾳ, whether supported by ς or not. I fancy therefore
that syr.*S* in Mark was translated from that ancient
Eastern text of which (in Mark) 1 &c 13 &c 565 are the
most consistent surviving Greek representatives. It may

---

[1] There is no tangible Syriac evidence for "after three days" in Lk., for
in Lk. ix 22 I am now convinced that *S* reads ⳨⳨⳨ ⳨⳨⳨⳨⳨, *lit.* "to
[*not*, after] three days," i.e. the same as in xxiv 7, 46, where τῇ τρ. ἡμ. is
certain.

be remarked that in Mk ix 31, x 34, syr.*S* (and syr.vg)
have a preposition which seems to suggest ἐν τῇ τρίτῃ
ἡμέρᾳ, like 28 in Mk viii 31.]

    7.  Mk x 50ᵇ ἀναπηδήσασ ℵBD 565 al latt[1]
          ἀναστὰσ ς syr.vg arm &c
          om. Γ syr.*S*

[I venture to think that this instance should not be
on the list. In Mk x 50ᵃ syr.*S* and aeth appear to support 565 in reading ἐπιβαλὼν for ἀποβαλών. Syr.*S* has
    "And he rose, took up his garments and came to Jesus."
Aeth has
    " And he rose and clothed himself with his clothing
and came...."
Obviously these agree exactly, probably because the
Ethiopic version was first made from the Syriac and
has only reached its present form by revision (? from
the Arabic). But the position of "rose" rather suggests that it is meant for ἐπι- in ἐπιβαλών. In any
case syr.*S* does not give a literal translation either of
the Syriac or of the Alexandrian and Western text of
the verse.]

    8.  Mk xii 5 πάλιν inserted.

[Here certainly syr.*S* tells us nothing. The Greek
has "4 And again he sent unto them another slave, and
him *they...and handled shamefully.* 5 *And he sent another,
and him* they killed...." It is the italicised portion
which is omitted in syr.*S*, by homoioteleuton of
κἀκεῖνον...κἀκεῖνον, so that it affords no evidence as to
the insertion or omission of πάλιν in *ver.* 5.]

    9.  Mk xv 8 ἀναβὰσ ℵBD *acffr*vg (hiant *bfnq*)
          sah boh goth

---

[1] N.B. *k* has exiuit, a misreading of exiliit, i.e. exsiliit. ·

ἀναβοήσασ ϛ syr.*S* -vg-hl-palest (*sic*) arm
om. *k*

[Here no doubt אB sah boh stand with D lat.eur and
syr.*S* stands with ϛ. But I feel inclined to believe that
ΑΝΑΒΟΗϹΑϹ is right and that ΑΝΑΒΑϹ is a mere corruption of
it. It is easier to derive ΑΝΑΒΑϹ from ΑΝΑΒΟΗϹΑϹ (by the
mere dropping of letters) than *vice versa*. In any case
it is noteworthy that *k* omits altogether: in how many
other cases is the apparent unanimity of Latin testimony
simply due to the absence of our best witness! I feel
convinced that our main ideas upon the grouping of
Gospel MSS. ought to be based on a study of those
passages where both *k* and syr.*S* are extant, i.e. on the
first half of St Matthew and the latter half of St Mark[1].]

Of this list of readings the three most striking are
Mk vii 5 ἔπειτα, Mk vii 14 πάντα, Mk xv 8 ἀναβοήσασ.
There is a good deal to be said for the originality of each
of these readings. Still it is a very small list, and deals
with very unimportant readings: what special conclusion
do you draw from it? A longer list of more important
agreements could be drawn up between (1) syr.*S* and
lat.vt, (2) syr.*S* and B or אB, (3) syr.*S* and members of
the groups 1 &c 13 &c 28 565 700. In all these cases
the trouble is to explain the genesis of the group that
supports the "wrong" reading. The "right" reading may
always be supposed to have accidentally escaped cor-
rection in any given line of transmission, but if we find
אBD or ϛאB united in error, then we have to imagine

---

[1] In Mk xv 11ᵃ is a noteworthy combination: for οἱ δὲ ἀρχιερεῖσ ἀνέσεισαν
τὸν ὄχλον we find οἵτινεσ καὶ τὸν ὄχλον ἔπεισαν in 565 (700) *a r* (syrᵖᵃˡᵉˢᵗ)
arm, 700 and syrᵖᵃˡᵉˢᵗ having ἀνέσεισαν with ϛ, no doubt by conflation.
The syrᵖᵃˡᵉˢᵗ is from some ancient fragments published by Dünsing (Göttingen,
1906).

a genealogical connexion of some kind between these groups. If ἀναβοήσασ in Mk xv 8 be really what the Evangelist wrote, then at this point אB and D lat.eur have a common ancestor later than the original. Similarly if (as I rather suppose) the true text of Mk vi 45 be εἰσ Βηθσαιδά, not εἰσ τὸ πέραν πρὸσ B., then ϛאBD latt must at this point have a common ancestor which introduced a harmonizing gloss from Matt. xiv 22, and (to name a better-known variant) all the authorities which read κῆνσον in Mk xii 14, instead of ἐπικεφάλαιον, must at that point have a common origin. I would say the same of the authorities which insert κατέστρεψεν in Mk xi 15, except that there may have been here several independent interpolations from Matt. xxi 12, Joh. ii 15.

My own feeling is that ϛ can practically be neglected, except as a source which contaminates the otherwise valuable later MSS., *viz.* 1 &c 13 &c 28 565 700. That there is a "geographically Eastern," i.e. non-Alexandrian, non-Western, element in syr.*S* is proved by the peculiar and isolated agreement of syr.*S* with *f* and *q* in Lk. xi 36, but here the grouping of the evidence is complicated by the fact that D lat.afr-eur syr.*C* simply assimilate to Matt. vi 23, and also by the fact that here ϛ sides with אB.

It seems to me that for St Mark, at least, Dr Hort's categories are too few, and (what is more serious) that we cannot be always sure that they are mutually independent. We have (1) אB generally with C*LΔ sah boh—an Alexandrian-Caesarean group; (2) D lat.afr-eur—a Western group; (3) a group 1 &c 13 &c 28 565 700—an Eastern group, so called, because readings of this group often agree with syr.*S* and we know that cod. 565 had some connexion with Pontus; (4) the

Antiochian or Syrian, an eclectic revision made in the 4th century. Of these (4) has often influenced the texts found in (3) and some of those in (1); possibly it may have influenced some of those reckoned to go with (2) here and there. There are old variations also within these groups.

If you take this classification, the number of triple variations increases, the typical case being Mk i 13. And the puzzle before the textual critic is to explain the historical meaning of combinations such as (1) + (2), (1) + (3), (2) + (3), whether (4) enters into them or not.

F. C. BURKITT.

# APPENDIX

## TRIPLE READINGS IN ST MATTHEW

I. 22. II. 9. III. 16. IV. 3, 23. V. 11, 30, 36, 39. VI. 25. VII. 10, 29.
VIII. 3, 28. IX. 18, 35. X. 3, 10, 19, 23. XI. 16. XII. 10, 18,
22, 25, 46. XIII. 28, 29, 52. XIV. 18, 19, 26, 34. XV. 1, 5, 6,
22. XVI. 5, 11, 20, 23. XVII. 14, 17, 26. XVIII. 2, 26. XIX. 4,
17, 22, 24, 26, 29. XX. 10, 17, 23, 30. XXI. 18. XXII. 5, 7, 30,
36, 43. XXIII. 14, 25. XXIV. 6, 7, 31, 44. XXV. 3, 15, 20.
XXVI. 44, 55, 71. XXVII. 23, 33, 41.

| | | |
|---|---|---|
| II. 9. (ϛ´ ·2) | ἐστάθη ἐπάνω οὗ ἦν τὸ παιδίον | A |
| | ἐσ. ἐπ. τοῦ παιδίου | W |
| | ἔστη ἐπ. οὗ ἦν τ. παιδίον | S |
| VI. 25. (μθ´ initium) | φάγητε | A |
| | φ. ἢ τί πίητε | W |
| | φ. καὶ τί πίητε | S |
| VII. 10. (νγ´ ·5) | ἢ καὶ ἰχθὺν | A |
| | ἢ ἐὰν ἰχ. | W |
| | καὶ ἐὰν ἰχ. | S |

68 *Appendix*

VII. 29. (ξβ′ finis)   οἱ γραμματεῖς αὐτῶν              A

οἱ γρ. αὐ. καὶ οἱ φαρισαῖοι              W

οἱ γρ.              S

VIII. 28. (ξθ′ ·5)   γαδαρηνῶν              A

γερασηνῶν              W

γεργεσηνῶν              S

X. 10. (πβ′ finis)   ἄξιος γὰρ ὁ ἐργάτης τῆς τροφῆς αὐτοῦ              A

Post γὰρ adde ἐστιν              W

Post αὐτοῦ adde ἐστιν              S

X. 19. (πη′ initium)   παραδῶσιν              A

παραδώσουσιν              W

παραδιδῶσιν              S

X. 23. (πθ′)   φεύγετε εἰς τὴν ἑτέραν              A

φ. εἰς τ. ἑτ.· κἂν ἐν τῇ ἑτέρᾳ διώκωσιν ὑμᾶς
φεύγετε εἰς τὴν ἄλλην              W

φ. εἰς τὴν ἄλλην              S

XII. 10. (ρις′ ·2)   ἄνθρωπος χεῖρα              A

ἄν. ἦν ἐκεῖ τὴν χ.              W

ἄν. ἦν τὴν χ.

XII. 22. (ριθ′)   τὸν κωφὸν                                           A

Omit                                                W

τὸν τυφλὸν καὶ τ. κωφὸν              S

XIII. 52. (ρμ′ finis)   μαθητευθεὶς τῇ βασιλείᾳ              A

μαθ. ἐν τ. βασ.                          W

μαθ. εἰς τὴν βασ.                        S

XIX. 17. (ρζγ′)   εἷς ἐστὶν ὁ ἀγαθός                              A

εἷς ἐσ. ὁ ἀγ. ὁ θεός                    W

οὐδεὶς ἀγαθὸς εἰ μὴ εἷς ὁ θεός       S

XX. 23. (σβ′ ′5)   λέγει αὐτοῖς                                         A

καὶ λ. αὐ. ὁ ιη̄ς̄                          W

καὶ λέγει αὐτοῖς                          S

XXIII. 13, 14. (σλα′ ′5)   13.  Οὐαὶ δὲ ὑμῖν, γραμματεῖς κ. φαρισαῖοι,
ὑποκριταί, ὅτι κατεσθίετε τὰς οἰκίας τῶν
χηρῶν κ. προφάσει μακρὰ προσευχό-
μενοι· διὰ τοῦτο λήψεσθε περισσότεραν
κρίμα

14.  Οὐαὶ ὑμῖν γραμ. κ. φαρ. ὑποκ. ὅτι
κλείετε τὴν βασιλείαν κ.τ.λ.

Omit *v.* 13                                              A

Reverse the verses          (Elzevir 1624) W

As above                    (Stephanus 1550) S

XXIV. 6.   (σμγ΄ ΄66)   δεῖ γὰρ γενέσθαι                                      A

      δ. γ. ταῦτα γεν.                              W

      δ. γ. πάντα γεν.                              S

XXIV. 7.   (σμγ΄ finis)   καὶ ἔσονται λιμοὶ                                   A

      κ. ἔσ. λοιμοὶ καὶ λιμοὶ                       W

      κ. ἔσ. λιμοὶ καὶ λοιμοὶ                       S

XXIV. 31.   (σνθ΄ ΄35)   μετὰ σάλπιγγος μεγάλης                               A

      μ. σάλ. καὶ φωνῆς μεγ.                        W

      μ. σ. φωνῆς μεγάλης                          S

XXV. 3.   (σξη΄ ΄25)   αἱ γὰρ μωραὶ                                          A

      αἱ δὲ μω.                                     W

      αἵτινες μωραὶ                                 S

XXV. 20.   (σο΄ ΄45)   ἐκέρδησα                                             A

      ἐπεκέρδησα                                   W

      ἐκέρδησα ἐπ' αὐτοῖς                          S

XXVII. 23.   (τκϛ΄)   ὁ δὲ ἔφη                                              A

      λέγει αὐτοῖς ὁ ἡγεμών·                       W

      ὁ δὲ ἡγεμὼν ἔφη                             S

XXVII. 41.   (τλη΄)   τῶν γραμματέων καὶ πρεσβυτέρων                          A

      τ. γραμ. καὶ φαρισαίων                       W

      τ. γρ. κ. πρεσ. καὶ φαρισαίων                S

# TRIPLE READINGS IN ST MARK

I. 4, 5, 13, 16, 18, 27, 31, 36, 37, 38, 40. II. 1, 3, 15, 21, 25, 26. III. 5, 6, 7, 19, 26, 34. IV. 10, 11, 16, 21, 25, 31, 37, 38. V. 1, 2, 9, 12, 15, 19, 23, 28, 33, 42. VI. 1, 3, 5, 15, 16, 25, 33, 34, 35, 43, 56. VII. 2, 8, 21, 24, 25, 28. VIII. 3, 5, 19, 25, 26, 28, 29. IX. 1, 3, 12, 15, 20, 38, 42, 43. X. 1, 4, 11, 12, 16, 20, 21, 27, 29, 32, 35, 46. XI. 6, 14, 24, 32, 33. XII. 2, 6, 14, 17, 28, 31, 38. XIII. 2, 5, 8, 10, 14, 19, 20, 25, 29, 30. XIV. 3, 4, 10, 18, 27, 35, 40, 51, 66, 68, 69, 72. XV. 12, 23, 35, 39, 40.

| I. 16. | (θ′ finis) | Σίμωνος | A |
| | | αὐτοῦ | W |
| | | αὐτοῦ τοῦ Σίμωνος | S |

| I. 16. | (θ′ finis) | ἐν τῇ θαλάσσῃ | A |
| | | τὰ δίκτυα ἐν τ. θαλ. | W |
| | | ἀμφίβληστρον ἐν τ. θ. | S |

| I. 38. | (ιζ′ ·5) | εἰς τοῦτο γὰρ ἐξῆλθον | A |
| | | ε. τ. γ. ἐλήλυθα | W |
| | | ε. τ. γ. ἐξελήλυθα | S |

II. 21.  (κγ΄ ΄7)      οὐδεὶς ἐπίβλημα                                           A

                        οὐ. δὲ ἐπ.                                               W

                        καὶ οὐ. ἐπ.                                             S


II. 21.  (κγ΄ ΄75)     τὸ πλήρωμα ἀπ᾽ αὐτοῦ τ. καινὸν τοῦ παλαιοῦ              A

                        τ. πλ. τὸ καινὸν ἀπὸ τ. παλ.                            W

                        τ. πλ. αὐτοῦ τ. κ. τ. παλ.                              S


II. 25.  (κδ΄ ΄5)      λέγει αὐτοῖς                                            A

                        εἶπεν αὐ.                                              W

                        ἔλεγεν αὐ.                                             S


III. 5.  (κε΄ finis)   ἡ χεὶρ αὐτοῦ                                           A

                        ἡ χ. α. ὑγιής                                          W

                        ἡ χ. α. ὑγιὴς ὡς ἡ ἄλλη                               S


III. 19. (λ΄ finis)    Ἰσκαριώθ                                               A

                        Σκαριώθ                                               W

                        Ἰσκαριώτην                                            S


III. 26. (λγ΄ ΄66)    στῆναι                                                  A

                        σταθῆναι ἡ βασιλεία αὐτοῦ                              W

                        σταθῆναι                                              S

| | | | |
|---|---|---|---|
| IV. 10. | (λϛ' finis) | τὰς παραβολάς. | A |
| | | τίς ἡ παραβολὴ αὐτή. | W |
| | | τὴν παραβολήν. | S |
| IV. 37. | (μζ') | ὥστε ἤδη γεμίζεσθαι τὸ πλοῖον | A |
| | | ὥστε γεμ. τ. πλ. | W |
| | | ὥστε αὐτὸ ἤδη γεμ. | S |
| V. 9. | (μζ' ·66) | λέγει αὐτῷ | A |
| | | ἀπεκρίθη | W |
| | | ἀπεκρίθη λέγων | S |
| V. 12. | (μζ' ·75) | λέγοντες | A |
| | | οἱ δαίμονες λέγ. | W |
| | | πάντες οἱ δαίμονες λέγ. | S |
| V. 42. | (μθ' finis) | ἐξέστησαν εὐθὺς | A |
| | | ἐξ. πάντες | W |
| | | ἐξέστησαν | S |
| VI. 1. | (ν' initium) | καὶ ἔρχεται | A |
| | | καὶ ἀπῆλθεν | W |
| | | καὶ ἦλθεν | S |

| VI. 3. (ν′ ·8) | καὶ Ἰωσῆτος | A |
| | κ. Ἰωσήφ | W |
| | κ. Ἰωσῆ | S |

| VI. 33. (ξβ′ finis) | καὶ προῆλθον αὐτούς | A |
| | κ. συνῆλθον αὐτοῦ | W |
| | κ. προῆλθον αὐτοὺς καὶ συνῆλθον πρὸς αὐτόν | S |

| VII. 28. (ογ′ ·5) | ναί, κύριε· καὶ τὰ κυνάρια | A |
| | κύριε· ἀλλὰ κ. τ. κυν. | W |
| | ναὶ κύριε· καὶ γὰρ τὰ κυν. | S |

| VIII. 3. (oϛ′ ·3) | καί τινες αὐτῶν | A |
| | ὅτι κ. τ. αὐ. | W |
| | τινες γὰρ αὐτῶν | S |

| VIII. 25. (πα′ ·75) | καὶ διέβλεψεν· καὶ | A |
| | κ. ἤρξατο ἀναβλέψαι· καὶ | W |
| | κ. ἐποίησεν αὐτὸν ἀναβλέψαι· καὶ | S |

| VIII. 26. (πα′ finis) | μηδὲ εἰς τὴν κώμην εἰσέλθῃς | A |
| | ὕπαγε εἰς τὸν οἶκόν σου, καὶ ἐὰν εἰς τ. κώμην εἰσέλθῃς μηδενὶ εἴπῃς μηδὲ ἐν τῇ κώμῃ | W |
| | μηδὲ ε. τ. κ. εἰσ. μηδὲ εἴπῃς τινὶ ἐν τῇ κώμῃ | S |

| | | | |
|---|---|---|---|
| X. 12. (ρε′) | καὶ ἐὰν αὐτὴ ἀπολύσασα τ. ἄνδρα αὐτῆς | A |
| | κ. ἐὰν γυνὴ ἐξέλθῃ ἀπὸ τ. ἀνδρὸς καὶ | W |
| | κ. ἐὰν γυνὴ ἀπολύσῃ τ. ἄνδρα αὐτῆς καὶ | S |
| | | |
| XI. 6. (ριη′ ·5) | εἶπεν | A |
| | εἰρήκει | W |
| | ἐνετείλατο αὐτοῖς | S |
| | | |
| XI. 14 (ρκ′ ·8) | ἀποκριθεὶς εἶπεν | A |
| | εἶπεν | W |
| | ἀπ: ὁ ι̅ς̅ εἶπεν | S |
| | | |
| XI. 24. (ρκε′) | ἐλάβετε | A |
| | λήψεσθε | W |
| | λαμβάνετε | S |
| | | |
| XIV. 10. (ρξ′ initium) | Ἰσκαριώθ | A |
| | Σκαριώτης | W |
| | Ἰσκαριώτης | S |
| | | |
| XIV. 27. (ρξη′) | σκανδαλισθήσεσθε, | A |
| | σκ. ἐν ἐμοί, | W |
| | σκ. ἐν ἐμοὶ ἐν τῇ νυκτὶ ταύτῃ | S |

# 76 *Appendix*

| XIV. 35. (ροε′) | ἔπιπτεν | A |
| | ἔπεσεν ἐπὶ πρόσωπον | W |
| | ἔπεσεν | S |
| XIV. 51. (ρπϛ′) | συνηκολούθει | A |
| | ἠκολούθει | W |
| | ἠκολούθησεν | S |
| XV. 40. (σκϛ′) | Ἰωσῆτος | A |
| | Ἰωσήφ | W |
| | Ἰωσῆ | S |

# TRIPLE READINGS IN ST LUKE

I. 28, 29, 37, 50, 56, 70.  II. 5, 15, 37, 48.  III. 16, 23, 30, 31, 32.
IV. 4, 8, 20, 35.  V. 2, 5, 12, 20, 25, 30.  VI. 2, 4, 8, 10, 16.
VII. 1, 28, 32, 33, 35, 46.  VIII. 12, 17, 20, 26, 30, 37.  IX. 8, 9,
20, 37, 43, 56, 57, 59, 62.  X. 2, 21, 27, 32, 37, 42.  XI. 11, 18,
27, 28, 37, 53.  XII. 28, 38, 47, 59.  XIV. 17, 33.  XV. 1, 10, 17,
26.  XVI. 4, 6, 9, 21, 29.  XVII. 9, 12, 33, 35.  XVIII. 4, 7, 11,
14, 24, 28, 30.  XIX. 4, 11, 15, 16, 22, 26, 42, 44, 45, 46.  XX. 2,
3, 14, 20, 24, 25, 30, 33, 40.  XXI. 13, 15, 30, 36.  XXII. 4, 6, 13,
22, 31, 48, 50, 54, 55, 62, 64, 66, 68.  XXIII. 2, 3, 8, 21, 36, 38,
39, 42, 46, 50, 53, 55.  XXIV. 1, 18, 20, 29, 32, 34, 36, 40, 47,
50, 53.

| | | |
|---|---|---|
| I. 56.  (α′ ′7) | ὡς μῆνας τρεῖς· | A |
| | μ. τρ. | W |
| | ὡσεὶ μῆνας τρ. | S |
| | | |
| II. 5.  (α′ finis) | ἐμνηστευμένη αὐτῷ | A |
| | αὐτῷ γυναικί | W |
| | μεμνηστευμένη αὐτῷ γυναικί | S |
| | | |
| II. 37.  (γ′ ′75) | ἕως ἐτῶν ὀγδοήκοντα | A |
| | ἐτ. ὀγδ. | W |
| | ὡς ἐτ. ὀγδ. | S |

| | | |
|---|---|---|
| v. 12.   (λγ΄ initium) | ἰδὼν δὲ τὸν ιν | A |
| | καὶ αὐτὸς | W |
| | καὶ ἰδ. τ. ιν | S |
| | | |
| v. 20.   (λζ΄ ΄3) | εἶπεν· ἄνθρωπε | A |
| | εἶπεν τῷ ἀνθρώπῳ | W |
| | εἶπεν αὐτῷ· ἄνθρωπε | S |
| | | |
| vi. 16.   (μδ΄ finis) | Ἰσκαριώθ | A |
| | Σκαριώθ | W |
| | Ἰσκαριώτην | S |
| | | |
| viii. 26.   (πγ΄ ΄33) | Γεργεσηνῶν | A |
| | Γερασηνῶν | W |
| | Γαδαρηνῶν | S |
| | | |
| ix. 10.   (ϟα΄) | εἰς πόλιν καλουμένην Βηθσαιδά. | A |
| | εἰς τόπον ἔρημον B. | W |
| | εἰς τόπον ἔρημον πόλεως καλουμένης B. | S |
| | | |
| ix. 43.   (ρ΄) | ἐποίει, | A |
| | ἐποίει, εἶπεν αὐτῷ ὁ Πέτρος· κύριε, διὰ τί ἡμεῖς οὐκ ἠδυνήθημεν ἐκβαλεῖν αὐτό; εἶπεν αὐτοῖς· τοῦτο γὰρ τὸ γένος προσ- ευχαῖς καὶ νηστείαις ἐκβάλλεται | W |
| | ἐποίησεν ὁ ις | S |

| | | | |
|---|---|---|---|
| IX. 57. | (ρε′ ·2) | καὶ πορευομένων | A |
| | | καὶ ἐγένετο πορ. | W |
| | | ἐγένετο δὲ πορ. | S |
| X. 2. | (ρη′) | ἔλεγεν δὲ | A |
| | | καὶ ἔλ. | W |
| | | ἔλ. οὖν | S |
| X. 27. | (ρκα′ ·5) | ἐν ὅλῃ τῇ διανοίᾳ | A |
| | | Omit | W |
| | | ἐξ ὅλης τῆς διανοίας | S |
| X. 32. | (ρκβ′ ·3) | κατὰ τὸν τόπον, ἐλθὼν | A |
| | | γενόμενος κ. τ. τ. | W |
| | | γεν. κ. τ. τ. ἐλθὼν | S |
| X. 37. | (ρκβ′ ·6) | εἶπεκ δὲ | A |
| | | καὶ εἶπεν | W |
| | | εἶπεν οὖν | S |
| X. 42. | (ρκβ′ finis) | ὀλίγων δέ ἐστιν χρεία ἢ ἑνός | A |
| | | Omit | W |
| | | ἑνὸς δέ ἐστιν χρεία | S |

| X. 42. (ρκβ′ finis) | Μαρία γὰρ | A |
| | M. | W |
| | M. δὲ | S |

| XI. 53. (ρμγ′) | κἀκεῖθεν ἐξελθόντος αὐτοῦ | A |
| | As below plus ἐνώπιον παντὸς τοῦ λαοῦ | W |
| | λέγοντος δὲ αὐτοῦ ταῦτα πρὸς αὐτούς | S |

| XII. 47. (ρνθ′) | καὶ μὴ ἑτοιμάσας ἢ ποιήσας | A |
| | κ. μ. ἑτ. | W |
| | κ. μὴ ἑτοιμάσας μηδὲ ποιήσας | S |

| XVIII. 7. (σιδ′ ·5) | καὶ μακροθυμεῖ | A |
| | μακροθυμῶν | W |
| | καὶ μακροθυμῶν | S |

| XVIII. 14. (σιε′) | παρ’ ἐκεῖνον | A |
| | μᾶλλον παρ’ ἐκεῖνον τὸν φαρισαῖον | W |
| | ἢ γὰρ ἐκεῖνος | S |

| XIX. 22. (σκθ′ ·66) | λέγει | A |
| | καὶ εἶπεν | W |
| | λέγει δὲ | S |

| | | | |
|---|---|---|---|
| XIX. 26. | (σλ′) | λέγω | A |
| | | λέγω δέ | W |
| | | λ. γάρ | S |
| XIX. 42. | (σλϛ′ ˙33) | πρὸς εἰρήνην | A |
| | | π. εἰ. σοι | W |
| | | π. εἰ. σου | S |
| XIX. 45. | (σλη′) | πωλοῦντας | A |
| | | π. καὶ ἀγοράζοντας κ. τὰς τραπέζας τ. κολλυβιστῶν ἐξέχεεν καὶ τὰς καθέδρας πωλούντων τ. περιστεράς | W |
| | | π. ἐν αὐτῷ καὶ ἀγοράζοντας | S |
| XX. 3. | (σμ′ ˙3) | λόγον | A |
| | | Omit | W |
| | | ἕνα λόγον | S |
| XX. 30. | (σμγ′ ˙5) | καὶ ὁ δεύτερος | A |
| | | κ. ἔλαβεν ὁ δεύτ. αὐτὴν κ. οὗτος ἀπέθανεν ἄτεκνος | W |
| | | κ. ἔλαβεν ὁ δ. τὴν γυναῖκα κ. οὗτος ἀπέθανεν ἄτεκνος | S |
| XX. 33. | (σμγ′ ˙66) | ἡ γυνὴ οὖν ἐν τῇ ἀναστάσει | A |
| | | ἐν τῇ ἀνασ. | W |
| | | ἐν τῇ οὖν ἀναστάσει | S |

H.                                                                                        6

| | | |
|---|---|---|
| xx. 40. (σμγ′ finis) | οὐκέτι γὰρ | A |
| | καὶ οὐκέτι | W |
| | οὐκέτι δὲ | S |
| | | |
| xxi. 15. (σνα′ ′33) | ἀντιστῆναι ἢ ἀντειπεῖν | A |
| | ἀντιστῆναι | W |
| | ἀντειπεῖν οὐδὲ ἀντιστῆναι | S |
| | | |
| xxii. 31. (σογ′) | Σίμων Σίμων | A |
| | εἶπε δὲ ὁ Κύριος Πετρῷ, Σ. Σ. | W |
| | εἶπε δὲ ὁ κ̄ς̄ Σ. Σ. | S |
| | | |
| xxii. 62. (σⳘδ′) | καὶ ἐξελθὼν ἔξω | A |
| | Omittit totum versum | W |
| | κ. ἐξ. ἔξω ὁ Πέτρος | S |
| | | |
| xxiii. 2. (τα′) | τὸ ἔθνος ἡμῶν | A |
| | τ. ἔθ. ἡμ. καὶ καταλύοντα τ. νόμον κ. τ. προφήτας | W |
| | τ. ἔθ. | S |
| | | |
| xxiii. 42. (τκς′ ′66) | μνήσθητί μου | A |
| | κύριε μν. μ. | W |
| | μν. μ. κύριε | S |

| XXIII. 46. (τκη΄) | τοῦτο δὲ | A |
| | καὶ τοῦτο | W |
| | καὶ ταῦτα | S |
| XXIII. 50. (τλβ΄) | καὶ ἀνὴρ ἀγαθὸς | A |
| | ἀγαθὸς | W |
| | ἀνὴρ ἀγ. | S |
| XXIV. 1. (τλϚ΄) | ἀρώματα | A |
| | Omit | W |
| | ἀρ. καί τινες σὺν αὐταῖς | S |
| XXIV. 32. (τλθ΄ ʹ75) | ὡς ἐλάλει ἡμῖν ἐν τῇ ὁδῷ ὡς διήνοιγεν | A |
| | ἐν τῇ ὁδῷ ὡς διήνοιγεν | W |
| | ὡς ἐλ. ἡ. ἐν τ. ὁδῷ καὶ ὡς διή. | S |
| XXIV. 40. (τμ΄ finis) | καὶ τοῦτο εἰπὼν ἔδειξεν αὐτοῖς τ. χεῖρας κ. τ. πόδας | A |
| | Omit | W |
| | Cum A sed ἐπέδειξεν | S |
| XXIV. 50. (τμβ΄ ʹ7) | ἕως πρὸς Βηθανίαν | A |
| | εἰς Β. | W |
| | ἕως εἰς Β. | S |
| XXIV. 53. (τμβ΄ finis) | εὐλογοῦντες | A |
| | αἰνοῦντες | W |
| | αἰν. κ. εὐλ. | S |

# TRIPLE READINGS IN ST JOHN

I. 19, 26, 27, 32, 39, 43, 50. II. 6, 17. V. 15, 37. VI. 10, 23, 24, 35,
40, 45, 57, 70, 71. VII. 12, 40, 46. VIII. 12, 33, 52. IX. 6, 8,
11, 17, 20, 25, 26, 30, 37, 41. X. 4, 12, 25, 31, 38, 39, 42.
XII. 1, 9, 13, 26, 47. XIII. 6, 8, 12, 23, 24, 25, 26, 38. XIV. 3, 5.
XV. 14, 26. XVI. 13, 19, 28. XVII. 22, 23. XVIII. 18, 22, 24,
29, 40. XIX. 4, 11, 15, 17, 28, 30, 33, 38. XX. 11, 21, 23.
XXI. 11, 15, 17.

| | | | |
|---|---|---|---|
| I. 27. (ιβ′) | ὁ ὀπίσω | | A |
| | αὐτός ἐστιν ὃν εἶπον ὁ ὀπίσω | | W |
| | αὐτός ἐστιν ὁ ὀπίσω | | S |
| II. 17. (κβ′) | ἐμνήσθησαν | | A |
| | καὶ ἐμν. | | W |
| | ἐμν. δὲ | | S |
| V. 37. (μδ′) | ἐκεῖνος μεμαρτύρηκεν | | A |
| | αὐτὸς μαρτύρει | | W |
| | αὐτὸς μεμαρτύρηκεν | | S |

| | | | |
|---|---|---|---|
| VI. 10. | (μθ′ ·ς) | εἶπεν | A |
| | | εἶπεν οὖν | W |
| | | εἶ. δὲ | S |
| VI. 35. | (νε′) | εἶπεν | A |
| | | εἶ. οὖν | W |
| | | εἶ. δὲ | S |
| VI. 40. | (νη′) | τοῦ πατρός μου, | A |
| | | τ. πέμψαντός με πατρός, | W |
| | | τ. πέμψαντός με, | S |
| VI. 45. | (ξ′ finis) | πᾶς ὁ ἀκούσας | A |
| | | π. ὁ ἀκούων | W |
| | | π. οὖν ὁ ἀκούων (vel ἀκούσας T.R.) | S |
| VI. 70. | (θε′) | ὁ ῑ̄ς̄ (T.R.) | A |
| | | ὁ ῑ̄ς̄ καὶ εἶπεν αὐτοῖς | W |
| | | Omit | S |
| VI. 71. | (θε′) | Ἰσκαριώτου | A |
| | | Σκαριώθ | W |
| | | Ἰσκαριώτην | S |

| | | | |
|---|---|---|---|
| VII. 40. | (πβ′) | ἐκ τοῦ ὄχλου οὖν | A |
| | | ἐκ τ. ὄχ. δὲ | W |
| | | πολλοὶ οὖν ἐκ τ. ὄχ. | S |
| | | | |
| IX. 6. | (πθ′ ·5) | ἐπὶ τοὺς ὀφθαλμούς | A |
| | | ἐπὶ τ. ὀφ. αὐτοῦ | W |
| | | ἐπὶ τ. ὀφ. τοῦ τυφλοῦ | S |
| | | | |
| IX. 8. | (πθ′ ·5) | προσαίτης ἦν | A |
| | | τυφλὸς καὶ προσ. ἦν | W |
| | | τυφλὸς ἦν | S |
| | | | |
| IX. 11. | (πθ′ ·5) | ἀπελθὼν οὖν | A |
| | | καὶ ἀπῆλθον | W |
| | | ἀπελθὼν δὲ | S |
| | | | |
| IX. 17. | (πθ′ ·55) | λέγουσιν οὖν | A |
| | | ἔλεγον οὖν | W |
| | | λέγουσιν | S |
| | | | |
| IX. 20. | (πθ′ ·6) | ἀπεκρίθησαν οὖν | A |
| | | ἀπ. (T.R.) | W |
| | | ἀπ. δὲ | S |

| IX. 25. | (πθ′ ·66) | ἀπεκρίθη οὖν ἐκεῖνος | A |
| | | εἶπεν οὖν ἐκεῖνος | W |
| | | ἀπ. οὖν ἐκ. καὶ εἶπεν | S |
| IX. 26. | (πθ′ ·66) | εἶπον οὖν | A |
| | | εἶπον | W |
| | | εἶπον δὲ | S |
| X. 4 (a). | (πθ′ ·85) | ὅταν | A |
| | | ὅτ. δὲ | W |
| | | καὶ ὅταν | S |
| X. 4 (β). | (πθ′ ·85) | τὰ ἴδια πάντα | A |
| | | τ. ἴδ. πρόβατα πάντα | W |
| | | τ. ἴδ. πρόβατα | S |
| X. 31. | (ϟβ′ ·6) | ἐβάστασαν πάλιν | A |
| | | ἐβ. οὖν | W |
| | | ἐβ. οὖν πάλιν | S |
| X. 38. | (ϟβ′ ·95) | ἵνα γνῶτε καὶ γινώσκετε | A |
| | | ἵνα γνῶτε | W |
| | | ἵνα γ. κ. πιστεύσητε | S |

| | | | |
|---|---|---|---|
| XII. 47. | (ριβ′ ΄3) | μὴ φυλάξῃ | A |
| | | φ. | W |
| | | μὴ πιστεύσῃ | S |
| | | | |
| XIII. 6. | (ριε′ ΄15) | αὐτῷ | A |
| | | αὐτῷ Πέτρος | W |
| | | αὐτῷ ἐκεῖνος | S |
| | | | |
| XIII. 12. | (ριε′ finis) | καὶ ἀνέπεσεν | A |
| | | κ. ἀναπεσὼν | W |
| | | ἀναπεσὼν | S |
| | | | |
| XIII. 26. | (ρκδ′) | Ἰσκαριώτου | A |
| | | Σκαριώθ | W |
| | | Ἰσκαριώτῃ | S |
| | | | |
| XV. 26. | (ρμε′ ΄4) | ὅταν ἔλθῃ | A |
| | | ὅταν οὖν ἔλ. | W |
| | | ὅταν δὲ ἔλ. | S |
| | | | |
| XVI. 19. | (ρμθ′ ΄5) | ἔγνω | A |
| | | ἔγ. δὲ vel καὶ ἔγνω | W |
| | | ἔγ. οὖν | S |

XVII. 22. (ρνγ΄ ΄66)    καθὼς ἡμεῖς ἕν·      A

                 καθ. καὶ ἡμ. ἕν ἐσμεν·    W

                 κ. ἡμ. ἕν ἐσμεν·    S


XVII. 23. (ρνγ΄ ΄9)    ἵνα γιν.      A

                 καὶ γιν.    W

                 καὶ ἵνα γιν.    S


XVIII. 40. (ρπδ΄)    πάλιν      A

                 πάντες    W

                 πάλιν πάντες    S


XIX. 4. (ρπϛ΄)    καὶ ἐξῆλθεν      A

                 ἐξῆλθεν    W

                 ἐξ. οὖν    S


XIX. 38. (σϛ΄)    τὸ σῶμα αὐτοῦ. (secundus)    A

                 αὐτόν.    W

                 τ. σ. τοῦ ιυ̅    S

# TRIPLE READINGS IN THE ACTS

I. 5, 23. II. 1, 6, 12, 38, 41. III. 13, 21. IV. 8, 12, 17, 32. V. 22, 39, 41, 42. VII. 16, 17, 18, 21, 31, 39. IX. 17, 26, 35, 43. X. 11, 12, 16, 23, 48. XI. 7, 12, 25. XII. 15, 22. XIII. 20, 31, 32, 35, 43 (a), 43 (β). XIV. 2, 7, 10, 17. XV. 1, 4, 7, 17, 18, 23, 28, 29, 36, 37. XVI. 7, 9, 11, 12, 39. XVII. 2, 10, 13, 14, 25, 27, 32. XVIII. 2, 7, 11, 19, 21. XIX. 4, 9. XX. 1 (a), 1 (β), 6, 16, 23, 25, 26, 28. XXI. 6, 14, 17, 20, 22. XXII. 2, 20, 26, 29, 30. XXIII. 7 (a), 7 (β), 9, 12, 20 (a), 20 (β), 23, 29, 34. XXIV. 17, 24, 27. XXV. 5, 6. XXVI. 1, 24. XXVII. 2, 16, 34, 41. XXVIII. 19.

II. 12. (Γ′ ·25)   διηποροῦντο, ἄλλος πρὸς ἄλλον   A

διηπόρουν, ἄλ. πρὸς ἄλλον ἐπὶ τῷ γεγονότι   W

διηπόρουν, ἄλλος πρὸς ἄλλον   S

II. 38. (Γ′ ·8)   Ἰησοῦ Χριστοῦ εἰς ἄφεσιν τ. ἁμαρτιῶν ὑμῶν   A

τοῦ κυρίου Ἰ. Χ. εἰς ἄφεσιν ἁμαρτιῶν   W

Ἰ. Χ. εἰς ἄφεσιν ἁμαρτιῶν   S

II. 41. (Γ′ ·9)   ἀποδεξάμενοι   A

ἀποδεξ. καὶ πιστεύσαντες   W

ἀσμένως ἀποδεξ.   S

| III. 13. (Δ΄ ΄33) | παρεδώκατε καὶ ἠρνήσασθε | A |
| | παρ. εἰς κρίσιν καὶ ἠρν. αὐτόν | W |
| | παρ. κ. ἠρν. αὐτόν | S |
| IV. 8. (Δ΄ ΄8) | πρεσβύτεροι | A |
| | πρεσ. τοῦ Ἰσραὴλ ἀκούσατε | W |
| | πρεσ. τοῦ Ἰσρ. | S |
| IV. 17. (E΄ initium) | εἰς τὸν λαόν, ἀπειλησώμεθα | A |
| | εἰς τ. λ. τὰ ῥήματα ταῦτα ἀπειλησώμεθα | W |
| | εἰς τ. λ. ἀπειλῇ ἀπειλησώμεθα | S |
| IV. 32. (E΄ ΄5) | ψυχὴ μία | A |
| | ψ. μ. καὶ οὐκ ἦν διάκρισις ἐν αὐτοῖς οὐδεμία | W |
| | ἡ ψ. μ. | S |
| V. 39. (ϛ΄ ΄9) | καταλῦσαι αὐτούς. | A |
| | κ. αὐτοὺς οὔτε ὑμεῖς οὔτε βασιλεῖς οὔτε τυράν- νοι· ἀπέχεσθαι οὖν ἀπὸ τῶν ἀνθρώπων τούτων | W |
| | κ. αὐτό. | S |
| V. 42. (ϛ΄ finis) | τὸν χ̅ν̅ ι̅ν̅ | A |
| | τὸν κύριον ι̅ν̅ χ̅ν̅ (vel minus χ̅ν̅) | W |
| | ι̅ν̅ τὸν χ̅ν̅ | S |

| | | | |
|---|---|---|---|
| VII. 17. | (H′ ·3) | ὡμολόγησεν ὁ θεὸς | A |
| | | ἐπηγγείλατο ὁ θ. | W |
| | | ὤμοσεν ὁ θ. | S |
| VII. 18. | (H ·3) | βασιλεὺς ἕτερος ἐπ᾽ Αἴγυπτον, ὃς οὐκ ᾔδει | A |
| | | βασ. ἕτ. ὃς οὐκ ἐμνήσθη | W |
| | | βασ. ἕτ. ὃς οὐκ ᾔδει | S |
| VII. 21. | (H′ ·33) | ἐκτεθέντος δὲ αὐτοῦ | A |
| | | ἐκτεθέντος δὲ αὐτοῦ παρὰ τὸν ποταμόν | W |
| | | ἐκτεθέντα δὲ αὐτόν | S |
| VII. 39. | (H′ ·33) | ἐστράφησαν ἐν ταῖς καρδίαις | A |
| | | ἐστ. ταῖς καρ. | W |
| | | ἐστ. τῇ καρδίᾳ | S |
| X. 16. | (IE′ ·3) | καὶ εὐθὺς ἀνελήμφθη | A |
| | | κ. ἀνελ. | W |
| | | κ. πάλιν ἀνελ. | S |
| X. 48. | (IE′ finis) | Ἰησοῦ Χριστοῦ | A |
| | | τοῦ κυρίου Ἰ. Χ. | W |
| | | τοῦ κυρίου | S |

| | | |
|---|---|---|
| XI. 7. (Ιϛ´ ·25) | ἤκουσα δὲ καὶ | A |
| | καὶ ἤκουσα | W |
| | ἤκουσα δὲ | S |
| XI. 12. (Ιϛ´ ·5) | μηδὲν διακρίναντα | A |
| | Omit | W |
| | μηδὲν διακρινόμενον | S |
| XI. 25. (Ιϛ´ ·95) | ἐξῆλθεν δὲ εἰς Ταρσὸν ἀναζητῆσαι Σαῦλον καὶ εὑρὼν ἤγαγεν εἰς ᾿Αντιόχειαν | A |
| | ἀκούσας δὲ ὁ Σαῦλος ἐστὶν εἰς Ταρσὸν ἐξῆλ-θεν ἀναζητῶν αὐτόν· καὶ ὡς συντυχὼν παρεκάλεσεν ἐλθεῖν εἰς ᾿Αντιόχειαν | W |
| | ἐξῆλθεν δὲ εἰς Ταρσὸν ὁ Βαρνάβας ἀναζητῆσαι Σαῦλον καὶ εὑρὼν αὐτὸν ἤγαγεν αὐτὸν εἰς ᾿Αντιόχειαν | S |
| XIII. 31. (Κ´ ·5) | οἵτινες νῦν εἰσὶν μάρτυρες | A |
| | οἵτινες ἄχρι νῦν ε. μ. | W |
| | οἵτινες εἰσὶν μαρ. | S |
| XIII. 32. (Κ´ ·5) | ἡμῶν ἀναστήσας ῑν | A |
| | ἡμ. ἀν. τὸν κύριον ῑν χ̄ν̄ (vel ῑν) | W |
| | αὐτῶν ἡμῖν ἀν. ῑν | S |
| XIII. 35. (Κ´ ·55) | διότι καὶ ἐν ἑτέρῳ | A |
| | Omit διότι | W |
| | διὸ καὶ ἐν ἑτέρῳ | S |

XIII. 43 (a).   (K′ ·8)   Βαρνάβᾳ, οἵτινες προσλαλοῦντες αὐτοῖς        A

                          Βαρ. ἀξιοῦντες βαπτισθῆναι οἵ. πρ. αὐ.         W

                          Βαρ. οἱ. πρ.                                   S


XIII. 43 (β).   (K′ ·8)   προσμένειν τῇ χάριτι τοῦ θεοῦ                 A

                          As A plus ἐγένετο δὲ καθ' ὅλης τῆς πόλεως
                          διελθεῖν τὸν λόγον τοῦ θεοῦ                   W

                          ἐπιμένειν τ. χ. τ. θ.                         S


XIV. 2.   (KA′ ·25)       οἱ δὲ ἀπειθήσαντες Ἰουδαῖοι ἐπήγειραν        A

                          οἱ δὲ ἀρχισυνάγωγοι τῶν Ἰουδαίων καὶ οἱ
                          ἄρχοντες τῆς συναγωγῆς ἐπήγαγον
                          αὐτοῖς διωγμὸν κατὰ τῶν δικαίων              W

                          οἱ δὲ ἀπειθοῦντες Ἰ. ἐπ.                      S


XIV. 10.   (KB′ ·1)       καὶ ἥλατο                                     A

                          καὶ εὐθέως παραχρῆμα ἥλατο                   W

                          καὶ ἥλλετο                                    S


XIV. 17.   (KB′ ·5)       καίτοι                                        A

                          καίγε                                         W

                          καίτοιγε                                      S


XV. 1.   (KΓ′ initium)    περιτμηθῆτε τῷ ἔθει τῷ Μωϋσέως               A

                          περ. καὶ τῷ ἔθει Μ. περιπατῆτε               W

                          περιτέμνησθε τ. ἔθει Μ.                       S

| | | |
|---|---|---|
| **xv. 4.**  (ΚΓ΄ ·1) | παρεδέχθησαν | A |
| | παρ. μεγάλως | W |
| | ἀπεδέχθησαν | S |
| | | |
| **xv. 7.**  (ΚΓ΄ ·2) | ζητήσεως γενομένης ἀναστὰς Πέτρος | A |
| | συνζητήσεως γ. ἀνέστησεν ἐν πνεύματι Π. | W |
| | συνζητήσεως γ. ἀν. Π. | S |
| | | |
| **xv. 18.**  (ΚΓ΄ ·5) | γνωστὰ ἀπ᾽ αἰῶνος | A |
| | γνωστὸν ἀπ᾽ αἰῶνος τῷ κυριῷ τὸ ἔργον αὐτοῦ | W |
| | γνωστὰ ἀπ᾽ αἰ. ἐστι τῷ θεῷ πάντα τὰ ἔργα αὐτοῦ | S |
| | | |
| **xv. 23.**  (ΚΓ΄ ·6) | γράψαντες διὰ χειρὸς αὐτῶν | A |
| | γρ. δ. χ. α. ἐπιστολὴν περιέχουσαν τάδε | W |
| | γ. δ. χ. α. τάδε | S |
| | | |
| **xv. 29.**  (ΚΓ΄ ·75) | αἵματος καὶ πνικτῶν καὶ πορνείας | A |
| | αἵμ. κ. πορ. | W |
| | αἵμ. κ. πνικτοῦ κ. πορ. | S |
| | | |
| **xvi. 11.**  (ΚΔ΄ ·33) | ἀναχθέντες δὲ | A |
| | τῇ δὲ ἐπαύριον ἀναχθέντες | W |
| | ἀναχθέντες οὖν | S |

XVI. 12. (ΚΔ΄ ΄33)   κἀκεῖθεν εἰς Φιλίππους   A

ἐκεῖθεν δὲ εἰς Φ.   W

ἐκεῖθέν τε εἰς Φ.   S

XVI. 39. (ΚΔ΄ finis)   παρεκάλεσαν αὐτούς, κ. ἐξαγαγόντες ἠρώτων
ἀπελθεῖν ἀπὸ τῆς πόλεως   A

παρ. αὐτοὺς ἐξελθεῖν εἰπόντες ἠγνοήσαμεν
τὰ καθ᾽ ὑμᾶς ὅτι ἔσται ἄνδρες δίκαιοι
καὶ ἐξαγαγόντες παρεκάλεσαν αὐτοὺς
λέγοντες ἐκ τῆς πόλεως ταύτης ἐξέλ-
θατε μήποτε πάλιν συνστράφωσιν
ἡμῖν ἐπικράζοντες καθ᾽ ὑμῶν   W

παρεκάλεσαν a. κ. ἐξ. ἠρ. ἐξελθεῖν ἀπὸ τ. π.   S

XVII. 2. (ΚΕ΄ initium)   διελέξατο   A

διελέχθη   W

διελέγετο   S

XVII. 13. (ΚΕ΄ ΄3)   καὶ ταράσσοντες τοὺς ὄχλους   A

κ. τ. τ. ὄχ. οὐ διελίμπανον   W

τοὺς ὄχλους   S

XVIII. 2. (ΚΖ΄ initium)   ἀπὸ τῆς Ῥώμης   A

ἀ. τ. Ῥ. οἱ κατῴκησαν εἰς τὴν Ἀχαΐαν   W

ἐκ τῆς Ῥώμης   S

XVIII. 7.   (KZ΄ ΄25)   μεταβὰς ἐκεῖθεν εἰσῆλθεν                                  A

μ. ἀπὸ τοῦ Ἀκύλα εἰσῆλθεν                                                      W

μ. ἐ. ἦλθεν                                                                    S


XVIII. 11.   (KZ΄ ΄3)   ἐκάθισεν δὲ                                            A

καὶ ἐκάθισεν ἐν Κορίνθῳ                                                        W

ἐκάθισέν τε                                                                    S


XVIII. 21.   (KZ΄ ΄75)   ἀνήχθη ἀπὸ τῆς Ἐφέσου κ. κατελθὼν εἰς
Καισαρίαν                                                                       A

τὸν δὲ Ἀκύλαν εἴασεν ἐν Ἐφέσῳ· αὐτὸς δὲ
ἀνενεχθεὶς ἦλθεν εἰς Καισάρειαν                                                W

καὶ ἀν. ἀπὸ τ. Ἐ. κ. κατ. εἰς Κ.                                              S


XIX. 4.   (KH΄ ΄1)   εἰς τὸν ιν                                                A

εἰς τὸν ιν χν                                                                  W

εἰς τὸν χν ιν                                                                  S


XIX. 9.   (KH΄ ΄25)   Τυράννου                                                A

Τ. ἀπὸ ὥρας πέμπτης ἕως δεκάτης                                               W

Τ. τινὸς                                                                      S


XX. 25.   (KΘ΄ ΄5)   κηρύσσων τὴν βασιλείαν                                    A

κ. τ. β. τοῦ ιν                                                               W

κ. τ. β. τοῦ θεοῦ                                                            S

H.                                                                            7

XXI. 17. (ΛΑ' ·25)    γενομένων δὲ ἡμῶν εἰς Ἱεροσόλυμα, ἀσμένως
ἀπεδέξαντο                                                    A

κἀκεῖθεν ἐξιόντες ἤλθομεν εἰς Ἱ. ὑπέδεξεν
τε ἡμᾶς ἀσμένως οἱ ἀδελφοὶ                          W

γεν. δὲ ἡ. εἰς Ἱ. ἀσ. ἐδέξαντο                        S


XXII. 20. (ΛΔ' ·33)    καὶ ὅτε ἐξεχύννετο τὸ αἷμα Στεφάνου τοῦ
μάρτυρός σου                                                A

κ. ὁ. ἐξ. τ. α. Σ. τ. πρωτομάρτυρός σου          W

κ. ὁ. ἐξέχειτο τ. α. Σ. τ. μ. σου                       S


XXII. 30. (ΛΓ' initium) ἔλυσεν αὐτὸν                              A

πέμψας ἔ. α.                                                   W

ἔ. α. ἀπὸ τῶν δεσμῶν                                     S


XXIII. 9. (ΛΓ' ·75)    τινὲς τῶν γραμματέων                      A

τινὲς                                                            W

γραμματεῖς                                                    S


XXIII. 34, 35. (ΛΔ' finis) ἀναγνοὺς δὲ καὶ ἐπερωτήσας ἐκ ποίας ἐπαρ-
χείας ἐστίν, καὶ πυθόμενος ὅτι ἀπὸ
Κιλικίας διακούσομαί σου, ὅταν               A

ἀναγνοὺς δὲ τὴν ἐπιστολὴν κ. ἐπερωτήσας
τὸν Παῦλον· ἐκ ποίας ἐπαρχίας εἶ;
ἔφη· κιλιξ. κ. πυθόμενος ἔφη· ἀκού-
σομαί σου ὅταν                                        W

ἀναγνοὺς δὲ ὁ ἡγεμὼν κ.τ.λ.                       S

xxv. 5. (Λϛ′ initium) ἐν τῷ ἀνδρὶ ἄτοπον          A

                       ἐν τ. ἀν. τούτῳ ἄτοπον        W

                       ἐν τ. ἀν. τούτῳ            S

xxv. 6. (Λϛ′ initium) ἡμέρας οὐ πλείους ὀκτὼ ἢ δέκα    A

                       ἡμέρας ὀ. ἢ δ.             W

                       ἡμ. πλ. ἢ δέκα             S

xxvii. 34. (ΛΗ′ ΄6) μεταλαβεῖν τροφῆς             A

                       μ. τινος τρ.               W

                       προσλαβεῖν τρ.           S

xxviii. 19. (Μ′ ΄25) κατηγορεῖν                  A

                       κατηγορῆσαι ἀλλ᾽ ἵνα λυτρώσωμαι τὴν
                                ψυχήν μου ἐκ θανάτου      W

                       κατηγορῆσαι              S

# TRIPLE READINGS FROM THE CATHOLIC EPISTLES

St James I. 12, 25, 26, 27.  II. 3, 10, 19, 23.  III. 3, 8, 12.  IV. 11, 14.  V. 7.
1 Peter II. 6, 12, 21.  III. 7, 8, 15.  IV. 3, 4.  V. 5.
2 Peter I. 4.  II. 17, 21.  III. 9.
1 John II. 27.  IV. 2, 12, 19.  V. 13.
2 John 13.
3 John 9, 13.
Jude 1, 3, 5, 15, 18.

## ST JAMES

| | | |
|---|---|---|
| I. 12. (A' '6) | ἐπηγγείλατο | A |
| | ἐπ. ὁ θεὸς | W |
| | ἐπ. ὁ κύριος | S |
| | | |
| I. 25. (B' '6) | καὶ παραμείνας, οὐκ ἀκροατὴς | A |
| | κ. παρ. ἐν αὐτῷ, οὐκ ἀκρ. | W |
| | κ. παρ. οὗτος οὐκ ἀκρ. | S |
| | | |
| I. 26. (B' '7) | εἴ τις δοκεῖ θρησκὸς εἶναι | A |
| | εἰ δέ τις κ.τ.λ. | W |
| | εἴ τις δ. θ. εἶναι ἐν ὑμῖν | S |

| I. 27. (B′ ′9) | θρησκία καθαρὰ κ. ἀμίαντος παρὰ τῷ θεῷ | A |
| | θρησκία δὲ καθ. κ.τ.λ. | W |
| | θ. κ. κ. ἀ. παρὰ θεῷ | S |
| II. 3. (Γ′ ′25) | ἢ κάθου ὑπὸ τὸ ὑποπόδιον | A |
| | ἢ κάθου ἐπὶ τ. ὑπ. | W |
| | ἢ κάθου ὧδε ὑπὸ τ. ὑπ. | S |
| II. 10. (Γ′ ′75) | τηρήσῃ | A |
| | πληρώσει | W |
| | τηρήσει | S |
| II. 23. (Δ′ ′75) | φίλος θεοῦ ἐκλήθη.  ὁρᾶτε ὅτι | A |
| | δοῦλος θεοῦ κ.τ.λ. | W |
| | φ. θ. ἐκ.  ὁρ. τοίνυν ὅτι | S |
| III. 12. (E′ ′33) | οὔτε | A |
| | οὕτως οὔτε | W |
| | οὕτως οὐδεμία πηγὴ | S |
| IV. 11. (E′ ′8) | ὁ καταλαλῶν ἀδελφοῦ ἢ κρίνων | A |
| | ὁ γὰρ καταλαλῶν κ.τ.λ. | W |
| | ὁ κ. ἀδ. καὶ κρίνων | S |
| IV. 14. (E′ ′9) | ποία ἡ ζωὴ ὑμῶν | A |
| | ποία γὰρ ἡ ζωὴ ἡμῶν | W |
| | ποία γὰρ ἡ ζωὴ ὑμῶν | S |

# 1 ST PETER

| | | | |
|---|---|---|---|
| II. 6. | (Γ′ ·5) | ἐν γραφῇ | A |
| | | ἡ γραφή | W |
| | | ἐν τῇ γραφῇ | S |
| IV. 3. | (E ·25) | ἀρκετὸς γὰρ | A |
| | | ἀρκετὸς γὰρ ὑμῖν | W |
| | | ἀρκ. γ. ἡμῖν | S |
| V. 11. | (H′ ·25) | τὸ κράτος | A |
| | | τὸ κράτος καὶ ἡ δόξα | W |
| | | ἡ δόξα κ. τὸ κράτος | S |

# 2 ST PETER

| | | | |
|---|---|---|---|
| II. 17. | (Γ′ ·8) | καὶ ὁμίχλαι | A |
| | | κ. ὁμίχλη | W |
| | | νεφέλαι | S |
| II. 21. | (Γ′ finis) | ὑποστρέψαι | A |
| | | εἰς τὰ ὀπίσω ἀνακάμψαι (vel ἐπιστρέψαι) | W |
| | | ἐπιστρέψαι | S |
| III. 9. | (Δ′ ·5) | μακροθυμεῖ εἰς ὑμᾶς | A |
| | | μ. δι’ ὑμᾶς | W |
| | | μ. εἰς ἡμᾶς | S |

## 1 ST JOHN

| | | | |
|---|---|---|---|
| IV. 2. (Δ′ ·8) | γινώσκετε | | A |
| | γινώσκομεν | | W |
| | γινώσκεται | | S |
| IV. 19. (ϛ′ ·25) | ἀγαπῶμεν | | A |
| | ἀγ. τὸν θεὸν | | W |
| | ἀγ. αὐτὸν | | S |
| V. 13. (ϛ′ ·9) | τοῖς πιστεύουσιν | | A |
| | οἱ πιστεύοντες | | W |
| | καὶ ἵνα πιστεύητε | | S |

## 2 ST JOHN

| | | | |
|---|---|---|---|
| 13. (B′ finis) | ἐκλεκτῆς | | A |
| | ἐκ. ἡ χάρις μεθ᾽ ὑμῶν | | W |
| | ἐκ. Ἀμήν | | S |

## 3 ST JOHN

| | | | |
|---|---|---|---|
| 9. (A′ ·7) | Ἔγραψά τι | | A |
| | Ἔγ. ἂν | | W |
| | Ἔγραψα | | S |

# *Appendix*

## ST JUDE

| | | | |
|---|---|---|---|
| 1. (A′ initium) | τοῖς ἐν θεῷ πατρὶ ἠγαπημένοις | | A |
| | τοῖς ἔθνεσιν τοῖς ἐν θ. κ.τ.λ. | | W |
| | τ. ἐν θ. π. ἡγιασμένοις | | S |
| 5. (A′ ʼ25) | Ἰησοῦς | | A |
| | ὁ θεός | | W |
| | ὁ κύριος | | S |
| 18. (Γ′ ʼ25) | τοῦ χρόνου | | A |
| | τῶν χρόνων | | W |
| | χρόνῳ | | S |

# TRIPLE READINGS IN ST PAUL'S EPISTLES

Rom. I. 29.  II. 14, 16.  III. 4, 28.  IV. 12.  VI. 11, 12, 15.  VII. 13,
    25.  VIII. 1, 11, 14, 23, 26, 38.  IX. 11, 20, 33.  X. 17.  XI. 13,
    17, 25, 26.  XII. 4, 20.  XIII. 12.  XIV. 3, 8, 9.  XV. 8, 16, 24 (a),
    24 (β), 27, 31.  XVI. 5, 6, 7, 18, 19, 20, 23.
1 Cor. I. 1, 25.  II. 2, 11.  III. 5.  IV. 17.  V. 5.  VI. 5, 10.  VII. 8,
    14, 18, 22, 28, 29, 31, 32, 37, 38.  VIII. 2, 7.  IX. 1, 2, 6, 7, 8,
    10, 15, 16, 18, 21, 22.  X. 2, 10, 11, 27.  XI. 24.  XII. 9, 12.
    XIII. 8, 10.  XIV. 7, 10, 18, 35, 37.  XV. 5, 12, 19, 39, 47, 50, 55.
2 Cor. I. 10.  II. 3.  III. 5, 9.  IV. 2, 6, 10.  VI. 4, 15, 16.  X. 8, 12.
    XI. 3, 6, 17, 21, 23, 32.  XII. 14, 15.  XIII. 4.
Gal. III. 14.  IV. 8.  V. 1, 19, 24.  VI. 15, 17.
Eph. II. 8.  III. 12, 21.  V. 5, 19, 21, 25, 28.  VI. 18, 21.
Phil. I. 8, 23, 28.  II. 4, 5.  III. 10, 12, 14, 16.
Col. III. 14, 18, 24.
1 Thess. III. 7.  V. 3.
2 Thess. II. 11.  III. 4, 6.
Hebrews III. 9.  V. 4.  VII. 14.  IX. 10.  X. 18.  XI. 11.  XII. 18, 28.
1 Tim. I. 12, 17.  V. 25.  VI. 7.
2 Tim. IV. 18.
Titus II. 7, 11.  III. 5.
Philemon 5, 11.

## ROMANS

I. 29.  (A′ '75)    ἀδικίᾳ πονηρίᾳ πλεονεξίᾳ κακίᾳ    A

                ἀδ. πλεον. κακ. πορνείᾳ    W

                ἀδ. πορνείᾳ πον. πλεον. κάκ.    S

| | | | |
|---|---|---|---|
| II. 14. | (Β΄ ·2) | ποιῶσιν, οὗτοι | A |
| | | ποιῇ οἱ τοιοῦτοι | W |
| | | ποίει vel ποιῇ οὗτοι | S |
| | | | |
| II. 16. | (Β΄ ·3) | διὰ χ̅υ̅ ι̅υ̅ | A |
| | | διὰ ι̅υ̅ χ̅υ̅ τοῦ κυρίου ἡμῶν | W |
| | | διὰ ι̅υ̅ χ̅υ̅ | S |
| | | | |
| III. 4. | (Γ΄ ·5) | πᾶς δὲ ἄνθρωπος ψεύστης, καθάπερ | A |
| | | πᾶς γὰρ. ἄν. ψ. καθὼς | W |
| | | π. δὲ ἄν. ψ. καθὼς | S |
| | | | |
| VI. 12. | (Ζ΄ ·5) | ὑπακούειν ταῖς ἐπιθυμίαις αὐτοῦ | A |
| | | ὑπ. αὐτῇ | W |
| | | ὑπ. αὐτῇ ἐν ταῖς ἐπ. αὐ. | S |
| | | | |
| VII. 13. | (Θ΄ ·6) | ἐμοὶ ἐγένετο θάνατος | A |
| | | ἐμ. θάν. | W |
| | | ἐμ. γέγονεν θ. | S |
| | | | |
| VIII. 1. | (Ι΄ ·9) | ἐν χ̅ρ̅ ι̅υ̅ | A |
| | | ἐν χ̅ρ̅ ι̅υ̅ μὴ κατὰ σάρκα περιπατοῦσιν | W |
| | | ἐν χ̅ρ̅ ι̅υ̅ μὴ κατὰ σάρκα περιπατοῦσιν ἀλλὰ κατὰ πνεῦμα | S |

| IX. 11. | (ΙΔ΄ ·3) | μηδὲ πραξάντων τι ἀγαθὸν ἢ φαῦλον, | A |
| | | ἢ πρ. τι ἀγ. ἢ κακόν, | W |
| | | μ. πρ. τι ἀγ. ἢ κακόν, | S |
| IX. 33. | (ΙΕ΄ ·15) | καὶ ὁ πιστεύων ἐπ᾿ αὐτῷ οὐ καταισχυνθήσεται | A |
| | | κ. ὁ πισ. ἐπ᾿ αὐ. οὐ μὴ καταισχυνθῇ | W |
| | | καὶ πᾶς ὁ π. ἐ. α. οὐ καταισχυνθήσεται | S |
| X. 17. | (ΙΕ΄ ·85) | διὰ ῥήματος $\overline{χυ}$ | A |
| | | δ. ρ. | W |
| | | δ. ρ. θεοῦ | S |
| XI. 13. | (Ι϶΄ ·3) | ἐφ᾿ ὅσον μὲν οὖν | A |
| | | ἐφ᾿ ὅσον | W |
| | | ἐφ᾿ ὅσον μὲν | S |
| XI. 17. | (Ι϶΄ ·5) | συνκοινωνὸς τῆς ῥίζης πιότητος | A |
| | | συνκ. τῆς πιότ. | W |
| | | συνκ. τ. ρ. καὶ πιότητος | S |
| XII. 20. | (ΙΖ΄ ·33) | ἀλλὰ ἐὰν | A |
| | | ἐὰν | W |
| | | ἐὰν οὖν | S |

| | | | |
|---|---|---|---|
| XIII. 12. | (ΙΖ΄ ΄6) | ἀποθώμεθα οὖν τὰ ἔργα τοῦ σκότους, ἐδυσώμεθα δὲ | A |
| | | ἀποβαλώμεθα οὖν τ. ἔ. τ. σκ. ἐνδ. δὲ (vel καὶ ἐνδυσώμεθα) | W |
| | | ἀποθώμεθα ο. τ. ἔ. τ. σκ. καὶ ἐνδ. | S |
| XV. 8. | (ΙΗ΄ ΄5) | λέγω γὰρ χ̄ν̄ | A |
| | | λ. γ. ῑ̄ν̄ χ̄ν̄ | W |
| | | λ. δὲ χ̄ν̄ ῑ̄ν̄ | S |
| XV. 31. | (ΙΘ΄ ΄3) | καὶ ἡ διακονία μου | A |
| | | κ. ἡ δωροφορία μου | W |
| | | καὶ ἵνα ἡ διακονία μου | S |
| XVI. 5. | (ΙΘ΄ ΄5) | ἀπαρχὴ τῆς Ἀσίας εἰς χ̄ν̄ | A |
| | | ἀπ. τ. Ἀσ. ἐν χ̄ῷ̄ | W |
| | | ἀπ. τ. Ἀχαΐας εἰς χ̄ν̄ | S |
| XVI. 6. | (ΙΘ΄ ΄5) | ἐκοπίασεν εἰς ὑμᾶς | A |
| | | ἐκ. ἐν ὑμῖν | W |
| | | ἐκ. εἰς ἡμᾶς | S |
| XVI. 7. | (ΙΘ΄ ΄55) | οἳ καὶ πρὸ ἐμοῦ γέγοναν ἐν χ̄ῷ̄ | A |
| | | τοῖς πρὸ ἐμοῦ ἐν χ̄ῷ̄ ῑ̄ῡ̄ | W |
| | | οἳ κ. π. ἐμ. γεγόνασιν ἐν χ̄ῷ̄ | S |
| XVI. 20. | (ΙΘ΄ ΄66) | ἡ χάρις τοῦ κυρίου ἡμῶν Ἰησοῦ μεθ᾽ ὑμῶν | A |
| | | Omit | W |
| | | ἡ χ. τ. κ̄ῡ̄ ἡμ. ῑ̄ῡ̄ χ̄ῡ̄ μ. ὑμῶν | S |

# 1 CORINTHIANS

A

| | | | |
|---|---|---|---|
| VII. 8. | (Δ΄ ΄2) | αὐτοῖς ἐὰν μείνωσιν | A |
| | | αὐ. ἐὰν οὕτως μ. | W |
| | | αὐ. ἐστιν ἐὰν μ. | S |
| VII. 14. | (Δ΄ ΄33) | ἐν τῷ ἀδελφῷ | A |
| | | ἐν τῷ ἀνδρὶ τῷ πιστῷ | W |
| | | ἐν τῷ ἀνδρὶ | S |
| VII. 22. | (Δ΄ ΄55) | ὁμοίως ὁ ἐλεύθερος | A |
| | | ὁμοίως δὲ καὶ ὁ ἐλ. | W |
| | | ὁμ. καὶ ὁ ἐλ. | S |
| VII. 28. | (Δ΄ ΄7) | ἐὰν δὲ καὶ γαμήσῃς | A |
| | | ἐ. δ. κ. λάβῃς γυναῖκα | W |
| | | ἐ. δ. κ. γήμῃς | S |
| VII. 32. | (Δ΄ ΄8) | πῶς ἀρέσῃ τῷ κυρίῳ | A |
| | | π. ἀρ. τῷ θεῷ | W |
| | | π. ἀρέσει τ. κ̄ω̄ | S |
| VII. 38. | (Δ΄ ΄95) | γαμίζων κρεῖσσον ποιήσει | A |
| | | γαμίζων κρ. ποιεῖ | W |
| | | ἐκγαμίζων κρ. ποιεῖ | S |

IX. 2.　(E′ initium)　οὔπω　　　　　　　　　　　A

　　　　　　　　　　οὐδέπω　　　　　　　　　　　　W

　　　　　　　　　　οὐδέπω οὐδὲν　　　　　　　　　S

IX. 1.　(E′ ·2)　Ἰησοῦν　　　　　　　　　　　　A

　　　　　　　　Χριστὸν Ἰησοῦν　　　　　　　　W

　　　　　　　　Ἰησοῦν Χριστὸν　　　　　　　　S

IX. 2.　(E′ ·2)　μου τῆς ἀποστολῆς ὑμεῖς ἐστὲ ἐν κυρίῳ　　A

　　　　　　　　τῆς ἐμῆς ἀποστολῆς ὑμεῖς ἐστέ　　　　W

　　　　　　　　τῆς ἐμῆς ἀποστολῆς ὑμεῖς ἐστὲ ἐν κ͞ω͞　　S

IX. 7.　(E′ ·25)　τὸν καρπὸν αὐτοῦ οὐκ ἐσθίει　　　　　A

　　　　　　　　τ. κ. α. οὐκ ἐσ. καὶ πίνει　　　　　　W

　　　　　　　　ἐκ τοῦ καρποῦ αὐ. οὐκ ἐσ.　　　　　S

IX. 10.　(E′ ·3)　ἐπ᾽ ἐλπίδι τοῦ μετέχειν　　　　　　A

　　　　　　　　τῆς ἐλπίδος αὐτοῦ μετέχειν　　　　W

　　　　　　　　τῆς ἐλπίδος αὐτοῦ μετέχειν ἐπ᾽ ἐλπίδι　　S

IX. 16.　(E′ ·4)　καύχημα· ἀνάγκη γάρ μοι ἐπίκειται· οὐαὶ
　　　　　　　　　γάρ　　　　　　　　　　　　　　A

　　　　　　　　χάρις· ἀν. γ. μ. ἐπ.· οὐαὶ γάρ　　　W

　　　　　　　　καύχημα· ἀν. γ. μ. ἐπ.· οὐαὶ δὲ　　S

| | | | |
|---|---|---|---|
| **X.** 10. | (E′ ′66) | μηδὲ γογγύζετε, καθάπερ | A |
| | | μ. γογγύζωμεν καθὼς | W |
| | | μ. γογγύζετε καθὼς | S |
| **X.** 27. | (E′ ′9) | εἴ τις καλεῖ ὑμᾶς τῶν ἀπίστων | A |
| | | εἴ τ. κ. ὑ. τ. ἀπ. εἰς δεῖπνον | W |
| | | εἰ δέ τις κ. ὑ. τ. ἀπ. | S |
| **XII.** 28. | (H′ ′35) | ἔπειτα χαρίσματα | A |
| | | χαρίσματα | W |
| | | εἶτα χ. | S |
| **XIII.** 8. | (H′ ′45) | πίπτει· εἶτα δὲ | A |
| | | ἐκπίπτει· εἶτα | W |
| | | ἐκπίπτει· εἶτα δὲ | S |
| **XIV.** 7. | (H′ ′6) | δῷ, πῶς γνωθήσεται | A |
| | | δῷ, πῶς γνώσθη | W |
| | | δίδω, πῶς γνωθήσεται | S |
| **XIV.** 10. | (H′ ′65) | τοσαῦτα, εἰ τύχοι, γένη φωνῶν εἰσὶν | A |
| | | εἰ τ. γ. φ. εἰσὶν | W |
| | | τοσ. εἰ τ. γ. φ. ἐστιν | S |

| | | |
|---|---|---|
| XIV. 18. (H′ ′75) | εὐχαριστῶ τῷ θεῷ | A |
| | εὐ. τ. θ. μου | W |
| | εὐ. τ. θ. ὅτι | S |
| XIV. 37. (H′ finis) | ὅτι κυρίου ἐστὶν ἐντολή | A |
| | ὅτι κ̄ῡ ἐστίν | W |
| | ὅτι κ̄ῡ εἰσὶν ἐντολαί | S |
| XV. 5. (Θ′ ′05) | ἔπειτα τοῖς δώδεκα | A |
| | καὶ μετὰ ταῦτα τ. δώ. | W |
| | εἶτα τ. δ. | S |
| XV. 47. (Θ′ ′55) | ὁ δεύτερος ἄνθρωπος ἐξ οὐρανοῦ | A |
| | ὁ δ. ἅ. ἐξ οὐρ. ὁ οὐράνιος | W |
| | ὁ δ. ἄν. ὁ κύριος ἐξ οὐρ. | S |
| XV. 50. (Θ′ ′6) | κληρονομῆσαι οὐ δύναται | A |
| | οὐ κληρονομήσουσιν | W |
| | κλ. οὐ δύνανται | S |

# St Paul's Epistles

113

## 2 CORINTHIANS

| | | | |
|---|---|---|---|
| II. 3. | (B′ ·6) | λύπην σχῶ | A |
| | | λύπην ἐπὶ λύπην ἔχω | W |
| | | λ. ἔχω | S |
| III. 9. | (Δ′ ·25) | περισσεύει ἡ διακονία τῆς δικαιοσύνης δόξῃ | A |
| | | περισσεύσει ἡ δ. τ. δ. ἐν δόξῃ | W |
| | | περισσεύει ἡ δ. τ. δ. ἐν δόξῃ | S |
| IV. 10. | (ϛ′ ·15) | τὴν νέκρωσιν τοῦ Ἰησοῦ | A |
| | | τ. ν. τ. χ͞υ ι͞υ | W |
| | | τ. ν. τοῦ κυρίου ι͞υ | S |
| VI. 16. | (Z′ ·9) | ἡμεῖς γὰρ ναὸς θεοῦ ἐσμὲν ζῶντος καθὼς εἶπεν | A |
| | | ὑμεῖς γὰρ ναὸς θεοῦ ἐστὲ ζῶντος λέγει γὰρ | W |
| | | ὑμεῖς γὰρ ναὸς θ. ἐστὲ ζῶντος καθὼς εἶπεν | S |
| X. 8. | (I′ ·45) | ἔδωκεν ὁ κύριος | A |
| | | ἔδ. ὁ θεός | W |
| | | ἔδ. ὁ κ͞ς ἡμῖν | S |
| XI. 21. | (IA′ ·6) | ἠσθενήκαμεν | A |
| | | ἠσθενήσαμεν ἐν τούτῳ τῷ μέρει | W |
| | | ἠσθενήσαμεν | S |
| XIII. 4. | (IA′ ·85) | ζήσομεν σὺν αὐτῷ | A |
| | | ζ. ἐν αὐτῷ | W |
| | | ζησόμεθα σὺν αὐτῷ | S |

H.

8

*Appendix*

## GALATIANS

v. 1. (Θ′ finis)    τῇ ἐλευθερίᾳ ἡμᾶς χρς ἠλευθέρωσεν. στήκετε
οὖν                                                  A

τῇ ἐλ. ἡμ. χρς ἠλ. στήκετε       W

τῇ ἐλ. οὖν ἡμ. χρς ἠλ. στήκετε    S

v. 24. (ΙΑ′ ·4)    οἱ δὲ τοῦ χυ ιυ τὴν σάρκα        A

οἱ δὲ τ. χυ τὴν σάρκα αὐτῶν     W

οἱ δὲ τ. χυ τὴν σάρκα          S

vi. 17. (ΙΑ′ finis)    τὰ στίγματα τοῦ Ἰησοῦ        A

τ. στ. τ. κυρίου                W

τ. στ. τ. κυ ιυ                 S

## EPHESIANS

ii. 8. (Γ′ ·4)    τῇ γὰρ χάριτί ἐστε σεσωσμένοι διὰ πίστεως    A

τῇ γὰρ αὐτοῦ χαρ. σέσ. ἐσμεν διὰ πίσ.    W

τῇ γ. χ. ἐστε σεσ. διὰ τῆς πίσ.         S

iii. 21. (Ε′ finis)    ἐν τῇ ἐκκλησίᾳ καὶ ἐν χρ ιης       A

ἐν χρ ιης καὶ ἐν τῇ ἐκκλησίᾳ      W

ἐν τ. ἐκκ. ἐν χρ ιης              S

| | | | |
|---|---|---|---|
| v. 19. | (H′ ·75) | τῇ καρδίᾳ | A |
| | | ἐν ταῖς καρδίαις | W |
| | | ἐν τῇ καρδίᾳ | S |
| v. 21. | (H′ finis) | ἐν φόβῳ χ̅υ̅ | A |
| | | ἐν φ. χ̅υ̅ ι̅υ̅ (vel ι̅υ̅ χ̅υ̅) | W |
| | | ἐν φ. θεοῦ | S |
| VI. 18. | (I′ ·5) | κ. εἰς αὐτὸ ἀγρυπνοῦντες | A |
| | | κ. εἰς αὐτὸν ἀγρ. πάντοτε | W |
| | | κ. εἰς αὐτὸ τοῦτο ἀγρ. | S |

## PHILIPPIANS

| | | | |
|---|---|---|---|
| I. 23. | (B′ ·75) | πολλῷ γὰρ μᾶλλον κρεῖσσον | A |
| | | ποσῷ γ. μ. κρ. | W |
| | | πολλῷ μ. κρ. | S |
| I. 28. | (Γ′ ·1) | ὑμῶν δὲ σωτηρίας | A |
| | | ἡμῖν δ. σ. | W |
| | | ὑμῖν δ. σ. | S |
| II. 4. | (I′ ·33) | ἕκαστοι (ultimus) | A |
| | | Omit | W |
| | | ἕκαστος | S |

| II. 5. (Γ΄ ΄4) | τοῦτο φρονεῖτε | A |
| | τ. γὰρ φρονεῖτε | W |
| | τ. γὰρ φρονείσθω | S |

| III. 10. (Ε΄ ΄5) | συνμορφιζόμενος | A |
| | συνφορτειζόμενος | W |
| | συμμορφούμενος | S |

| III. 14. (Ε΄ ΄66) | εἰς τὸ βραβεῖον τῆς ἄνω κλήσεως τοῦ θεοῦ | A |
| | ἐπὶ τ. βρ. τ. ἄ. κλ. | W |
| | ἐπὶ τ. βρ. τ. ἄ. κλ. τ. θ. | S |

| III. 16. (Ε΄ ΄75) | τῷ αὐτῷ στοιχεῖν | A |
| | τῷ αὐτῷ φρονεῖν τῷ αὐτῷ κανόνι στοιχεῖν | W |
| | τ. αὐ. στ. κανόνι τὸ αὐτῷ φρονεῖν | S |

## COLOSSIANS

| III. 14. (Θ΄ ΄8) | ὅ ἐστιν σύνδεσμος τῆς τελειότητος | A |
| | ὅ (vel ὅς) ἐστιν σ. τ. ἑνότητος | W |
| | ἥτις ἐ. σ. τ. τελ. | S |

| III. 18. (Ι΄ ΄1) | ὑποτάσσεσθε τοῖς ἀνδράσιν | A |
| | ὑπ. τοῖς ἀνδ. ὑμῶν | W |
| | ὑπ. τοῖς ἰδίοις ἀνδ. | S |

| | | | |
|---|---|---|---|
| III. 24. | (Ι΄ ΄3) | τῷ κυρίῳ χριστῷ δουλεύετε | A |
| | | τοῦ κ̄ῡ (ἡμῶν ῑῡ) χ̄ῡ ᾧ δουλ. | W |
| | | τῷ γὰρ κ̄ρ̄ῳ̄ χ̄ρ̄ῳ̄ δουλ. | S |

## 1 THESSALONIANS

| | | | |
|---|---|---|---|
| III. 7. | (Β΄ ΄8) | ἐπὶ πάσῃ τῇ ἀνάγκῃ καὶ θλίψει | A |
| | | ἐν πάσῃ τῇ ἀν. κ. θλ. | W |
| | | ἐπὶ πάσῃ τῇ θλίψει καὶ ἀνάγκῃ | S |

## 2 THESSALONIANS

| | | | |
|---|---|---|---|
| II. 11. | (Β΄ ΄9) | καὶ διὰ τοῦτο πέμπει | A |
| | | διὰ τ. π. | W |
| | | κ. δ. τ. πέμψει | S |
| III. 6. | (Ε΄ initium) | παρελάβοσαν | A |
| | | παρελάβετε | W |
| | | παρέλαβον | S |

## HEBREWS

| | | | |
|---|---|---|---|
| III. 9. | (Δ΄ ΄5) | ἐν δοκιμασίᾳ | A |
| | | ἐδοκίμασαν | W |
| | | ἐδοκίμασάν με | S |

v. 4.   (ϛ′ ·66)        καθώσπερ καὶ                                    A

                        καθώσπερ                                        W

                        καθάπερ καὶ                                     S

IX. 10.  (ΙΑ′ finis)    δικαιώματα                                      A

                        δικαίωμα                                        W

                        δικαιώμασιν                                     S

X. 1.   (ΙΒ′ ·9)        οὐδέποτε δύνανται τοὺς προσερχομένους
                            τελειῶσαι                                   A

                        οὐ. δύναται τ. πρ. καθαρίσαι                     W

                        οὐ. δύναται τ. π. τελ.                          S

XI. 11.  (Ιϛ′ ·3)       ἔλαβεν καὶ παρὰ καιρὸν ἡλικίας                  A

                        ἔλ. εἰς τὸ τεκνῶσαι (καὶ) παρὰ κ. ἡλ.          W

                        ἔλ. κ. π. κ. ἡλ. ἔτεκεν                         S

XII. 18. (ΙΘ′ initium)  ψηλαφωμένῳ καὶ                                  A

                        ψηλ.                                            W

                        ψηλ. ὄρει                                       S


# 1 TIMOTHY

I. 17.  (Β′ finis)      ἀφθάρτῳ ἀοράτῳ μόνῳ θεῷ                         A

                        ἀθανάτῳ ἀοράτῳ μ. θ.                            W

                        ἀφ. ἀορ. μόνῳ σοφῷ θεῷ                          S

v. 25.  (ΙΔ′ initium)    πρόδηλα                              A

                         πρ. εἰσίν                           W

                         πρ. ἐστιν                           S


VI. 7.  (Ις′ ′4)         εἰς τὸν κόσμον, ὅτι                  A

                         εἰς τ. κ. ἀληθὲς ὅτι                W

                         εἰς τ. κ. δῆλον ὅτι                 S


## 2 TIMOTHY

IV. 18.  (Θ′ ′75)        ῥύσεταί με ὁ κύριος                 A

                         ἐρρύσατό με ὁ κ̄ς̄                    W

                         καὶ ῥύσεταί με ὁ κ̄ς̄                S


## TITUS

II. 7.  (Γ′ ′75)         ἀφθορίαν                            A

                         ἀφθ. ἁγνείαν                       W

                         ἀδιαφθορίαν                         S


II. 11.  (Δ′ ′33)        τοῦ θεοῦ σωτήριος                   A

                         τ. θ. τοῦ σωτῆρος ἡμῶν             W

                         τ. θ. ἡ σωτήριος                   S

## PHILEMON

| | | |
|---|---|---|
| *v.* 5. (A′ ʼ25) | ἀγάπην καὶ τὴν πίστιν ἣν ἔχεις εἰς | A |
| | πίστιν κ. τ. ἀγάπην ἣν ἔχ. εἰς | W |
| | ἀγ. κ. τ. πίσ. ἣν ἔχ. πρὸς | S |
| *v.* 11. (B′ ʼ1) | ὃν ἀνέπεμψά σοι | A |
| | ὃν ἔπεμψά σοι | W |
| | ὃν ἀνέπεμψα | S |

# TRIPLE READINGS IN THE APOCALYPSE

I. 4, 9, 13. II. 7, 10, 20. III. 2, 7, 16, 18. IV. 3, 7, 11. V. 1, 2, 3.
VI. 5, 8, 9, 11. VIII. 5, 12. IX. 10, 11, 14, 15. X. 2, 9, 10, 11.
XI. 6, 10, 19. XII. 2, 3. XIII. 16. XIV. 1, 6, 8, 10. XVI. 3, 4,
17. XVII. 3, 4, 8. XVIII. 3, 4, 12, 14. XIX. 6, 17. XX. 5, 8,
9, 12. XXI. 3, 5, 10, 23, 27. XXII. 5.

| | | | |
|---|---|---|---|
| I. 4. (Aʹ ·4) | τῶν ἐνώπιον | | A |
| | ἃ ἐστὶν ἐν. | | W |
| | ἃ ἐν. | | S |
| I. 9. (Bʹ initium) | ἐν ιης vel ἐν χρ | | A |
| | ιης χρ | | W |
| | ἐν χρ. ιης | | S |
| I. 13. (Bʹ ·5) | τῶν λυχνιῶν | | A |
| | τ. (ἑπτὰ) λυχ. τῶν χρυσῶν | | W |
| | τ. ἑπτὰ λυχνιῶν | | S |
| II. 20. (ϛʹ ·25) | ἡ λέγουσα | | A |
| | τὴν λέγουσαν | | W |
| | ἡ λέγει | | S |

| | | | |
|---|---|---|---|
| III. 2. | (Ζ′ ·3) | ἀποθανεῖν | A |
| | | ἀποθνήσκειν | W |
| | | ἀποβάλλειν | S |
| III. 7. | (Η′ initium) | καὶ κλείων | A |
| | | καὶ κλείει | W |
| | | εἰ μὴ ὁ ἀνοίγων | S |
| III. 18. | (Θ′ ·6) | ἔγχρισαι | A |
| | | ἔγχρισον | W |
| | | ἵνα ἐγχρίσῃ | S |
| IV. 7. | (Ι′ ·66) | ὡς ἀνθρώπου | A |
| | | ὡς ἄνθρωπος | W |
| | | ἀνθρώπου | S |
| IV. 11. | (Ι′ finis) | ὁ κύριος κ. ὁ θεὸς ἡμῶν | A |
| | | κύριε ὁ θεὸς ἡμῶν | W |
| | | ὁ κύρ. κ. ὁ θ. ἡμ. ὁ ἅγιος | S |
| IX. 11. | (Κϛ′ ·9) | ἔχουσιν | A |
| | | καὶ ἔχουσιν | W |
| | | ἔχουσαι | S |

IX. 14.  (ΚΖ´ ·2)  λέγοντα                    A

                   λέγουσαν                   W

                   λέγοντος                   S


X. 2.   (ΚΗ´ ·2)  βιβλαρίδιον                 A

                  βιβλιδάριον                 W

                  βίβλιον                     S


XI. 10.  (Λ´ finis)  πέμψουσιν                A

                     πέμπουσιν                W

                     δώσουσιν                 S


XI. 19.  (ΛΓ´ initium)  καὶ σεισμὸς          A

                        καὶ σεισμοὶ          W

                        Omit                 S


XII. 2.  (ΛΓ´ ·4)  κράζει                     A

                   ἔκραζεν                    W

                   ἔκραξεν                    S


XIV. 10.  (ΜΒ´ ·4)  τῶν ἀγγέλων              A?

                    ἀγγέλων ἁγίων            W?

                    τῶν ἁγίων ἀγγέλων        S

| XVI. 3. (MZ′ finis) | ζωῆς | A |
| | ζῶσα | W |
| | Omit | S |
| | | |
| XVI. 17. (NB′ initium) | ναοῦ | A |
| | οὐρανοῦ | W |
| | ναοῦ τοῦ οὐρανοῦ | S |
| | | |
| XVII. 3. (NΓ′ ·5) | γέμοντα ὀνόματα | A |
| | γέμον ὀνομάτων | W |
| | γέμον ὀνόματα | S |
| | | |
| XVIII. 3. (NE′ 15) | ἐκ τοῦ θυμοῦ | A |
| | ἐκ τοῦ θυμοῦ τοῦ οἴνου | W |
| | ἐκ τοῦ οἴνου τοῦ θυμοῦ | S |
| | | |
| XVIII. 4. (NE′ ·2) | ἐξέλθατε | A |
| | ἐξέλθετε | W |
| | ἔξελθε | S |
| | | |
| XVIII. 14. (NE′ ·6) | εὑρήσουσιν | A |
| | εὑρήσεις | W |
| | εὕρῃς | S |

| | | | |
|---|---|---|---|
| XIX. 8. | (NZ´ ·25) | λαμπρὸν καθαρόν. | A |
| | | καθ. καὶ λαμπρόν. | W |
| | | λαμ. καὶ καθ. | S |
| | | | |
| XIX. 17. | (NH´ ·6) | ἕνα ἄγγελον | A |
| | | ἄλλον ἄγγελον | W |
| | | ἄγγελον | S |
| | | | |
| XX. 9. | (ΞΓ´ ·66) | ἐκ τοῦ οὐρανοῦ | A |
| | | ἀπὸ τοῦ θεοῦ ἐκ τ. οὐρ. | W |
| | | ἐκ τ. οὐρ. ἀπὸ τ. θεοῦ | S |
| | | | |
| XXI. 5. | (ΞϚ´ initium) | πιστοὶ καὶ ἀληθινοὶ εἰσίν | A |
| | | ἀλ. κ. πισ. εἰσίν | W |
| | | ἀλ. κ. πιστ. εἰσὶν τοῦ θεοῦ | S |
| | | | |
| XXII. 5. | (ΞΗ´ finis) | οὐκ ἔσται ἔτι | A |
| | | οὐκ ἔσται ἐκεῖ | W |
| | | οὐκ ἔσται | S |

FINIS

For EU product safety concerns, contact us at Calle de José Abascal, 56–1°, 28003 Madrid, Spain or eugpsr@cambridge.org.

www.ingramcontent.com/pod-product-compliance
Ingram Content Group UK Ltd.
Pitfield, Milton Keynes, MK11 3LW, UK
UKHW012332130625
459647UK00009B/246